ESTHER

A WOMAN OF DISCRETION AND VALOR

Study by Ronnie McBrayer
Commentary by Brett Younger

Free downloadable Teaching Guide for this study available at
NextSunday.com/teachingguides

NextSunday Resources
6316 Peake Road
Macon, Georgia 31210-3960
1-800-747-3016
©2013 by NextSunday Resources

TABLE OF CONTENTS

Esther: A Woman of Discretion and Valor

HOW TO USE THIS STUDY

NextSunday Resources Adult Bible Studies are designed to help adults study Scripture seriously within the context of the larger Christian tradition and, through that process, find their faith renewed, challenged, and strengthened. We study the Scriptures because we believe they affect our current lives in important ways. Each study contains the following three components:

Study Guide

Each study guide lesson is arranged in four movements:

Reflecting recalls a contemporary story, anecdote, example, or illustration to help us anticipate the session's relevance in our lives.

Studying is centered on giving the biblical material in-depth attention while often surrounding it with helpful insights from theology, ethics, church history, and other areas.

Understanding helps us find relevant connections between our lives and the biblical message.

What About Me? provides brief statements that help unite life issues with the meaning of the biblical text.

Commentary

Each study guide lesson is accompanied by an additional, in-depth commentary on the biblical material. Written by a different author than the study guide, each commentary gives the opportunity for learners to approach the Scripture text from a separate but complementary viewpoint.

Teaching Guide

In addition to the provided study guide and commentary, *NextSunday Resources* also provides a *free* downloadable teaching guide, available at NextSunday.com. Each teaching guide gives the teacher tools for focusing on the content of each study guide lesson through additional commentary and Bible background information. Through teacher helps and teaching options, each teaching guide also provides substance for variety and choice in the preparation of each lesson.

NextSunday
Resources

STUDY INTRODUCTION

Some five centuries before Christ, the biblical narrative travels east, out of Israel to the kingdom of Persia—modern-day Iran. King Ahasuerus, or Xerxes, ruled the Middle East and the Persian Gulf at the apex of world domination. God's people, the Jews, were in exile, yanked violently away from their homeland. There, in a foreign land, one of the great stories of Jewish deliverance unfolds, precipitated by a beautiful young woman named Esther.

The account that bears Esther's name is one of the more enigmatic books of the Old Testament. Once part of the *Kethubim* or "miscellaneous writings" of Judaism, it was one of the last books admitted into the canon of Scripture, and only then with editorial adjustment. Why the delay? First, a clear candidate for authorship has never emerged. More importantly, God is not mentioned anywhere in the entire volume. This is a unique characteristic of Esther when compared to the other biblical writings. Nevertheless, this appears to be the author's intent, whoever he or she may have been: invoked or not invoked, God is present.

The book of Esther is not a record of historical facts as such. Rather, it is a magnificent narrative that refuses to interpret life as being driven by coincidence or happenstance. While the silence of God is all too normative for life, this does not mean God is not nearby or actively at work behind the scenes. In the otherwise unknown characters of Esther, Haman, and Mordecai, we trace the movement of the divine hand as God collaborates with God's risk-taking people to rescue them from the hand of their enemies.

At the conclusion of the book of Esther, the reader is introduced to the Jewish festival of Purim. This was a national celebration honoring the Jewish deliverance from extermination. The word Purim means "chance" or "lot": the rolling of the dice. Yet, this escape from destruction was not the accomplishment of a lucky political wager. It was through the providence of God and the courage of the Jewish queen Esther.

THE KING
CHOOSES ESTHER

Esther 2:1-18

Central Question

When is it acceptable to keep my faith to myself?

Scripture

Esther 2:1-18 1 After these things, when the anger of King Ahasuerus had abated, he remembered Vashti and what she had done and what had been decreed against her. 2 Then the king's servants who attended him said, "Let beautiful young virgins be sought out for the king. 3 And let the king appoint commissioners in all the provinces of his kingdom to gather all the beautiful young virgins to the harem in the citadel of Susa under custody of Hegai, the king's eunuch, who is in charge of the women; let their cosmetic treatments be given them. 4 And let the girl who pleases the king be queen instead of Vashti." This pleased the king, and he did so. 5 Now there was a Jew in the citadel of Susa whose name was Mordecai son of Jair son of Shimei son of Kish, a Benjaminite. 6 Kish had been carried away from Jerusalem among the captives carried away with King Jeconiah of Judah, whom King Nebuchadnezzar of Babylon had carried away. 7 Mordecai had brought up Hadassah, that is Esther, his cousin, for she had neither father nor mother; the girl was fair and beautiful, and when her father and her mother died, Mordecai adopted her as his own daughter. 8 So when the king's order and his edict were proclaimed, and when many young women were gathered in the citadel of Susa in custody of Hegai, Esther also was taken into the king's palace and put in custody of Hegai, who had charge of the women. 9 The girl pleased him and won his favor, and he quickly provided her with her cosmetic treatments and her portion of food, and with seven chosen maids from the king's palace, and advanced her and her maids to the best place in the harem. 10 Esther did not reveal her people or kindred, for Mordecai had charged her not to tell. 11 Every day Mordecai would walk around in front of the court of the harem, to learn how Esther was and how she fared. 12 The turn came for each girl to go in to King Ahasuerus, after being twelve months under the regulations for the women, since this was the regular period of their cosmetic treatment, six months with oil of myrrh and six months with perfumes and cosmetics for women. 13 When the girl went in to the king she was given whatever she asked for to take with her from the harem to the king's palace. 14 In the evening she went in; then in the morning she came back to the second harem in custody of Shaashgaz, the king's eunuch, who was in charge of the concubines; she did not go in to the king again, unless the king delighted in her and she was summoned by name. 15 When the turn came for Esther daughter of Abihail the uncle of Mordecai, who had adopted her as his own daughter, to go in to the king, she asked for nothing except what Hegai the king's eunuch, who had charge of the women, advised. Now Esther was admired by all who saw her. 16 When Esther was taken to King Ahasuerus in his royal palace in the tenth month, which is the month of Tebeth, in the seventh year of his reign, 17 the king loved Esther more than all the other women; of all the virgins she won his favor and devotion, so that he set the royal crown on her head and made her queen instead of Vashti. 18 Then the king gave a great banquet to all his officials and ministers—"Esther's banquet." He also granted a holiday to the provinces, and gave gifts with royal liberality.

Reflecting

A traveler's vehicle broke down along the side of the road. After waving about wildly for half an hour, the man finally convinced a speeding motorist to stop and help. "If you could just use your car to push mine at a speed of forty miles per hour," the stranded motorist said to his newly arrived partner, "I'm convinced it will start and I'll be on my way." Sliding back behind the wheel of his car, the driver was relieved. The ordeal of being stuck in the middle of nowhere was over. He would be rolling again in a matter of seconds.

He waited for that gentle nudge on the rear bumper that would move him down the road. It never came. Looking around he discovered that his "Good Samaritan" had disappeared. What a cruel joke! Where could he have gone? It was then that he saw him in the rear-view mirror. His rescuer was a quarter of a mile away, bearing down on the broken-down car at forty miles per hour! The driver had not communicated as clearly as he had intended.

We Christians tend to make a habit of bumbling our communication. In these harrowing days when fewer and fewer people seem to stop and listen to us, we sometimes think the answer is to scream louder through picket signs, petitions, and displays of righteous indignation accompanied by red faces and bulging arteries. The result is indeed clearer communication: it is clear we are really mad about something.

Maybe holding to faith has an alternative side that opts for silence rather than screaming. It is sometimes more appropriate to be quiet about faith than to shout about it.

Studying

The book of Esther is set in the middle of the fifth century BC. The Jewish nation had been scattered throughout the Middle East and Persian Gulf, the result of successive invasions by the Assyrians, Babylonians, and Persians. The result was the destruction of the Jerusalem temple and the Davidic monarchy in Jerusalem and the deportation of thousands of Jews.

Cyrus the Great was the Persian king who conquered Babylonia and its former territories, including Judah. In the first year of his reign, he reversed the policy of forced deportation and allowed the Jewish people to return to their homeland. The events of the book of Esther take place some sixty years after this exile ended. Xerxes, called Ahasuerus in the book of Esther, was the grandson of Cyrus the Great and the king of Persia during Esther's time (486–465 BC).

The edict of Cyrus did not mean all Jews returned to their homeland. Many did not, having sunk roots into foreign soil and built homes and lives there. Esther is one such Jew, a third-generation deportee who had never lived in Israel (vv. 5–7). Her presence in Persia, and her striking beauty, are quickly recognized in the story.

Ahasuerus's wife, Queen Vashti, had refused to obey the kings' command that she appear at a party celebrating his reign. This public act of disrespect is narrated in Esther 1. In anger, the king banished Vashti from the kingdom. Her place was vacated and the royal counselors called for a kingdom-wide beauty contest to find her replacement (vv. 2–4). Esther was declared the winner and made queen of Persia (vv. 17–18).

Esther's king "Ahasuerus" is traditionally identified with Xerxes I of Persia (486–465), best known for his ill-fated invasion of the Greek mainland in the early years of his reign. Ahasuerus (Hebrew Achashverosh) is a variation on the Babylonian form of Khshayarsha, Xerxes' original Persian name.

The author of the book of Esther makes a subtle appeal to divine providence. Vashti's disrespect toward King Ahasuerus, coupled with his angry response and Esther's rise to prominence, are not intended to be viewed as coincidences. Rather, these events appear to communicate a divinely ordered chain of events. The author doesn't directly describe God's role in these events; it is simply understood. Adding to the divine suspense, Esther does not reveal her nationality to the king. Mordecai, her patron, guardian, and cousin, "had charged her not to tell" (v. 10).

Esther's identity remaining a secret is essential to the plot of the story. Revealing her Jewish heritage too early would defuse the tension, making the story largely ineffective. But it is worth

our time to consider *why* Mordecai advised Esther to hide her Jewish identity.

It could be that Mordecai is attempting to protect Esther. It might have appeared scandalous for a Persian king to marry a Jewish woman, like English royalty marrying a commoner. At the same time, many in the Jewish priesthood would not have received this marriage well. Many looked upon intermarriage with non-Israelites as the reason for much of the Jews' suffering during the exile. Furthermore, to marry a foreigner might be seen as giving in to the totalitarian imperial policies of the Assyrian-Babylonian past. Intermarriage destroyed tribal identities and allegiances.

> According to Herodotus, the Persian king could only marry a woman from one of seven noble families. The account of Esther hiding her family origins could explain how a commoner could marry into royalty.

The most likely reason Mordecai advised Esther to hide her ethnicity was pure common sense. At this juncture, it simply was not necessary to make her ethnic and religious identity known. It was more appropriate to allow providence to take its course, again betraying the dominant theme of the book's author: God may not be heard or seen, yet the Divine cannot be ignored. Mordecai likely harbored the hope that the two allegiances of Esther—to God and to the king—would not come into conflict.

Mordecai appears unwilling for Esther to short-circuit any future opportunity by acting boldly too soon. As readers privy to the end of the story, we know that Esther is neither ashamed of her identity nor lacking in bravery. Mordecai advises her to practice good judgment in addition to courage.

> The book of Esther has hit the silver screen! Well, almost. Rodrigo Santoro plays Xerxes, the biblical Esther's husband King Ahasuerus, in the 2007 release of *300*. The movie highlights the Persian invasion of Greece and the battle of Thermopylae in 480 BC.

A historical wrinkle in the narrative might also have driven Mordecai's wisdom. It is likely that after Vashti's removal, but before Esther's ascension, Ahasuerus waged a doomed, unsuccessful battle against the Greeks. The royal advisors who led the king to find a new and beautiful wife did not necessarily do

so because the king was lonely. Rather, they did so because his ego and his kingdom stung from defeat. The coronation of a new queen was just the sort of thing all of Persia needed.

Understanding

The book of Esther underscores God's subtlety in working in people's lives. Often we would love to see God put on a pyrotechnic display of power, parting the waters, writing the divine name in the sky, or setting the burning bush on fire for all to see. As we know, God rarely, if ever, does such sensational acts these days. Instead, God conceals the divine presence. God peeks and hides, always present but not always visible. Ironically, Esther fulfills a similar vocation.

As the newly crowned queen, she might have been tempted to use her position to advance her personal faith and cultural background. But Esther, listening to Mordecai, needed to know that restraint, and being comfortable with faith that works behind the scenes, would be the wisest path to take.

Remaining committed to our faith doesn't mean we should always wear it like a chip on our shoulder, being easily offended and quick to preach and correct others. Faithfulness is frequently best expressed quietly, respectfully, and even in silence. Clear communication is possible, even without words.

This story also reminds us that not all believers have the liberty of living in a nation where publicly articulating faith is acceptable. Hundreds of millions of non-Western Christians live in places where their religious freedoms are restricted, if not violated. In places like these, silence is more than tactful sensitivity; it is the only practical means of survival.

Have you ever lived or traveled in a country where overt displays of Christian faith were forbidden (or at least deemed unwise)? How do believers adapt to living in such circumstances? What temptations might they face that are different from those of believers in countries that enjoy religious freedom?

What About Me?

• *Sharing faith with others involves more than reciting Bible verses or rehearsed outlines.* Sharing one's faith is more about how a person lives than the church they attend or how many gospel tracts they distribute. It is an exciting challenge for us to fashion creative, alternative ways of sharing our faith. Living in a changing world requires imagination.

• *How our witness is heard is even more important than what we say.* Not everyone we meet is prepared to hear about Jesus or the Christian faith. Hurtful religious experiences, forced church attendance as a child, and philosophical differences can all be barriers. It takes much time, compassion, and skill to share our faith in situations where there could be forceful opposition. The one to whom we witness is more significant than the words we share.

• *People should never have faith forced upon them.* Anytime a person is forced, manipulated, or otherwise coerced into making a decision about faith, that person has suffered the greatest indignity. Faith is not a bludgeon with which to abuse others. Coercion of a spiritual decision shows no concern for another's spiritual well-being. When choosing between the need to "deliver the news" and respect for our hearers, we must opt for respect.

• *When circumstances dictate silence, we often reflect how God works in our lives.* God doesn't always act in obvious or noticeable ways. The name of God is not even mentioned in the book of Esther. God chooses to work behind the scenes. God's ways are never explained in Esther, but God is always assumed to be there. Sharing faith requires this God-like quality. As believers we are obligated to gain the wisdom to know when to speak and when to remain silent.

Resources

Tim Downs, *Finding Common Ground* (Chicago: Moody, 1999).

Stanley Hauerwas and William H. Willimon, *Where Resident Aliens Live* (Nashville: Abingdon, 1996).

David S. and John B. Noss, *A History of the World's Religions*, 9th ed. (New York: MacMillian, 1994).

THE KING CHOOSES ESTHER

Esther 2:1-18

Questionable Ways to Find a Wife

If a young person asks you how to find a spouse, think twice before suggesting the Old Testament for guidance. Boaz bought a piece of land and secured a wife as part of the deal. Jacob worked for seven years for a wife, but then got tricked into marrying the wrong woman. Hosea thought God told him to marry a prostitute. Deuteronomy 21 suggests a man can see a beautiful prisoner of war, take her home, shave her head, pare her nails, give her new clothes, wait a month while she grieves the death of her parents, and then marry her. In Judges 21, the elders recommend the young men of Benjamin's tribe go to a party and hide, then, "when the young women of Shiloh come out to dance," they should grab one and carry her off to be married. These approaches make King Ahasuerus's beauty contest seem almost reasonable.

The announcement reads like an advertisement for a television series like *The Bachelor*:

> The search is on for eligible women! Do you have the beauty, charm, and style to be the next queen of seduction? Interested, gorgeous, and submissive women should contact pageant producers to learn more about our competition.

Clearly, the book of Esther is not the best place to learn about the process of courtship.

I. The Stubborn King Removes the Stubborn Queen (1:1-12)

The first word in Esther is translated "This happened in the days of." This was the fifth century BC version of "Here comes a great story." The book of Ruth starts with the same word.

King Ahasuerus is usually identified with the Persian monarch Khshayarsha, known in the west as Xerxes, who reigned 486–465 BC. His invasion of Greece was slowed by the Spartans at Thermopylae and defeated at Salamis.

The historical questions surrounding Esther are hotly debated. Views range from the traditional opinion that the book is a precise and exact recounting of historical events, to the feeling that it is a story that should begin "Once upon a time." As is often the case, the truth probably falls between the extremes.

No historical information contradicts the history in Esther, and the story of attempted genocide is certainly possible. There are a few minor discrepancies in what various historians claim, however. For example, the histories of Esther's day list Ahasuerus's queen as Amestris. Neither Vashti nor Esther is mentioned outside the Bible. The book of Esther includes inspired, sacred, creative writing that builds on historical facts (George L. Murphy, "Providence and Passion in Esther," *Currents in Theology in Mission* 29/2 [April 2002]: 122–23).

The story begins with King Ahasuerus deciding to throw a party big enough to make Mardi Gras look like a deacons' meeting. Big-time kings love to throw big-time parties. Ahasuerus invites not only everybody who is anybody, but everybody who is nobody, too.

Ahasuerus is so rich that he can afford feasts of unimaginable length and extravagance that take place on floors constructed of costly materials. Porphyry (1:6), for instance, is a hard purplish-red rock quarried in ancient Egypt that contains small crystals of feldspar. This is what they were wiping their sandals on.

The author of Esther has an eye for detail, evidenced by the description of "white cotton curtains and blue hangings tied with cords of fine linen" (1:6). Silver couches were moved in by the cartload.

The king even made an imperial edict (1:8) to let the guests know that they could drink as much as they wanted. It wasn't long before the men were drinking straight from the pure gold pitchers. While the men enjoyed the world's most expensive keg party, Queen Vashti hosted a wine and cheese gathering for the wives.

By the time the seventh day rolled around, the king decided it was time to show off his queen. Vashti was quite a beauty, and he wanted to see the envy of the guests as he paraded her around. He sent messengers to tell her to come quickly.

Some rabbis interpreted that the command for Vashti to appear wearing her royal crown meant she was required to wear *only* her crown. This may be an overstatement, but the interpreters were correct in reading the offensiveness of Ahasuerus's actions.

Vashti is the overlooked heroine in this story. She refused to be paraded like a plaything in front of the king's fraternity brothers. She declined to be part of the drunken revelry. She was a human being and not a silver couch or a gold pitcher. She might have given up her crown, but she kept her self-respect.

II. Keeping Women in their Place? (1:13-22)

Ahasuerus was furious. Not only was he insulted, but if he allowed Vashti to get away with her defiance, what might the women want next? Every wife in Persia would soon know that Queen Vashti refused her husband's request. The men worried about keeping their wives in the proper place. They had to squash any hint of women's equality.

As one of the king's sages, Memucan instructed him on the ways of the law regarding Vashti's actions. Basically, he said, "King, with all due respect, if the queen gets away with this, every man in Persia will face similar defiance from their wives. Pick a new queen. You can find a better woman. If you do this, then throughout the whole kingdom women will honor their husbands as they should."

Ahasuerus divorced Vashti on the spot. Politicians are asking for trouble when they start making pronouncements about the balance of power between wives and husbands, but the king sent out a royal decree that men should rule their households (1:22). This edict ensured that all of the emperor's subjects were swiftly informed of Ahasuerus's inability to control his own household. The curious assertion, "let it be written among the laws of the Persians and the Medes so that it may not be altered" (1:19), is evidence that the book contains satirical elements, since such a policy would be practically unworkable.

III. Miss Persia Contest (2:1-18)

The king sent out a royal decree that "beautiful young virgins" should sign up immediately for the inaugural "Miss Persia" contest—a yearlong affair involving a spa, beauticians, and special diets. The beauty of Ahasuerus's replacement wife would surpass that of the original.

The Jews living in Persia were far from home and the temple. Three generations back, Mordecai's family was among the exiles taken from Jerusalem by Nebuchadnezzar of Babylon. He had raised his orphaned cousin Hadassah, or Esther.

Mordecai and his adopted daughter inhabited competing empires, the kingdom of Ahasuerus and the kingdom of God. Their dual citizenship is symbolized by the two names they each bear. To the empire, they were Mordecai and Esther, loyal citizens with conventional Persian names who were thoroughly conformed to their culture. Mordecai is a Hebraized form of the Babylonian name *marduka*, which includes within it the name of the Babylonian god Marduk. Esther is a Persian name, "star" (perhaps also with an allusion to the pagan goddess, *Ishtar*). At home, however, they were Mordecai *the Jew* and Hadassah, a Hebrew name meaning "Myrtle." Like many exiles, they lived their daily lives as citizens of two separate communities (Iain Duguid, "The Eschatology of the Book of Esther," *Westminster Theological Journal* 68 [2006]: 86–90).

Aside from the kidnapping of contestants like Esther, this was a first-rate pageant. Six months of beauty oils were followed by six months of perfume. Mary Kay should have been the corporate sponsor!

Mordecai's advice to Esther bordered on deceit. He told her not to tell anyone she was a Jew. He knew that if the truth got out, it might be the end for both of them. She kept her Judaism a secret. There is no mention of Esther attempting to maintain

Jewish religious customs such as kosher food regulations. With help from Hegal, the supervisor of the harem, she used her sex appeal to win the approval of King Ahasuerus. Perhaps there is a reason many Christians have attended church faithfully for a lifetime without participating in a Bible study on Esther. Martin Luther had a point when he complained about the "pagan naughtiness" in the book.

After Esther "went in to the king," he knew he had found the winner. He immediately scheduled a press conference to introduce the new queen.

IV. Keeping Quiet

The Jews faced difficult questions living as subjects under Gentile rule. On Mordecai's advice to conceal her Jewish identity, Esther lived such a conforming lifestyle that even her closest companions were unaware of her Jewishness. She lived as an assimilated Jew who accepted marriage with a Gentile and seemed willing to integrate fully into Persian society. It appears that only the threatened annihilation of her people aroused Esther's concern for Jewish identity.

It was impossible to follow the Mosaic Law without people noticing, so Esther chose not to follow the law. When faced with the same decision, heroes like Daniel, Meshach, Shadrach, and Abednego did not hide who they were.

Before we are too critical of Esther's decision to keep quiet, we should think about times when we keep our faith to ourselves. There are certain subjects we don't mention around certain friends. Not telling the truth can begin to feel like lying.

When do you talk? When do you keep quiet?

Do you tell a visitor from Boston that you're a New York Yankees fan?

Do you hide your love for hamburgers from your vegetarian friend?

Do you mention to your opinionated neighbor that you voted for the *other* candidate?

Do you admit to your mother-in-law that you've never liked her butternut squash?

Do you tell your favorite environmentalist that you love Nascar?

Do you inform your grandmother in Nashville that you've always hated country music?

Do you mention to a college student that English majors never make any money?

Do you inform your pal at the Ford plant that you bought a Toyota?

Do you let your boss know that no one likes his racist jokes?

Do you tell your barber that you pray for him?

Do you tell your coworker that he would enjoy visiting your Sunday school class?

Do you tell your cousin whose life is falling apart that God cared for you through a hard time?

Do you tell your friends that the most important person in your life is Jesus Christ?

Sharing our faith is hard. Most of us find it difficult. Sometimes we avoid telling the truth because we're afraid to offend someone, and there are times when perhaps silence is optimal. Even so, true Christianity calls us to share who we are without putting down those who disagree. Christians learn to be honest without being judgmental.

It was impossible for Esther to live as a Jew without people noticing. It should be just as impossible for us to live as Christians without people noticing.

Notes

Notes

2

MORDECAI
ANGERS HAMAN

Esther 3:1-15

Central Question

How am I responsible for others' reactions?

Scripture

Esther 3:1-15 1 After these things King Ahasuerus promoted Haman son of Hammedatha the Agagite, and advanced him and set his seat above all the officials who were with him. 2 And all the king's servants who were at the king's gate bowed down and did obeisance to Haman; for the king had so commanded concerning him. But Mordecai did not bow down or do obeisance. 3 Then the king's servants who were at the king's gate said to Mordecai, "Why do you disobey the king's command?" 4 When they spoke to him day after day and he would not listen to them, they told Haman, in order to see whether Mordecai's words would avail; for he had told them that he was a Jew. 5 When Haman saw that Mordecai did not bow down or do obeisance to him, Haman was infuriated. 6 But he thought it beneath him to lay hands on Mordecai alone. So, having been told who Mordecai's people were, Haman plotted to destroy all the Jews, the people of Mordecai, throughout the whole kingdom of Ahasuerus. 7 In the first month, which is the month of Nisan, in the twelfth year of King Ahasuerus, they cast Pur—which means "the lot"—before Haman for the day and for the month, and the lot fell on the thirteenth day of the twelfth month, which is the month of Adar. 8 Then Haman said to King Ahasuerus, "There is a certain people scattered and separated among the peoples in all the provinces of your kingdom; their laws are different from those of every other people, and they do not keep the king's laws, so that it is not appropriate for the king to tolerate them. 9 If it pleases the king, let a decree be issued for their destruction, and I will pay ten thousand talents of silver into the hands of those who have charge of the king's business, so that they may put it into the king's treasuries." 10 So the king took his signet ring from his hand and gave it to Haman son of Hammedatha the Agagite, the enemy of the Jews. 11 The king said to Haman, "The money is given to you, and the people as well, to do with them as it seems good to you." 12 Then the king's secretaries were summoned on the thirteenth day of the first month, and an edict, according to all that Haman commanded, was written to the king's satraps and to the governors over all the provinces and to the officials of all the peoples, to every province in its own script and every people in its own language; it was written in the name of King Ahasuerus and sealed with the king's ring. 13 Letters were sent by couriers to all the king's provinces, giving orders to destroy, to kill, and to annihilate all Jews, young and old, women and children, in one day, the thirteenth day of the twelfth month, which is the month of Adar, and to plunder their goods. 14 A copy of the document was to be issued as a decree in every province by proclamation, calling on all the peoples to be ready for that day. 15 The couriers went quickly by order of the king, and the decree was issued in the citadel of Susa. The king and Haman sat down to drink; but the city of Susa was thrown into confusion.

Reflecting

I struck up a conversation with a man at the coffee shop the other day. He was an extremely nice guy. We talked about the usual neighborly stuff: the weather, the news, work. When he discovered I was a Christian, he could not have been more delighted. He too was a person of deep faith. When he found out I was a minister, he was ecstatic. My perspective on beliefs and faith became the only topic to which he wanted to speak. This always makes me feel somewhat uncomfortable. It is the reason I am sometimes slow to reveal my vocation. I'm not ashamed of my faith or what I do for a living—not in the least. But when some people find out that you are of the pastoral persuasion (a reverend, preacher, or another type of minister), it becomes something like a press conference, as they pepper you with a million questions like "Where did Cain get his wife?"

Or, as with my newfound coffee companion, they squeeze you unmercifully into a preconceived, sanctified container. They assume that you, as a minister, spend all your time reading Old Testament Hebrew, watching the *700 Club*, and polishing your halo. To debunk this myth the best I could, I began talking about a recent movie I had seen. That was a mistake.

It was a movie with an "R" rating, and I was informed that such a transgression did not promote "family values." Further, in the course of our chat, I revealed that I had seen the movie on a Sunday afternoon: on the Lord's Day! This was more than my cappuccino-sipping friend could understand.

He was scandalized and fiercely confronted me: "What if Jesus had returned while you, a minister, were in that movie house on the Christian Sabbath? What would you have done if Jesus had walked in and sat down beside you?" I didn't mean to offend him, but needless to say, our conversation came to a screeching conclusion.

Studying

As Esther 2 closes, things are quiet in the Persian Empire. Esther grows into her new role as queen of Persia. Ahasuerus continues his domination of the Middle East. Mordecai maintains his valuable place in the bureaucracy, and life is comfortable for the Jews living outside of their homeland. This status quo is maintained for nearly four years (compare Esth 2:16 with Esth 3:7).

Then, a new character appears in the narrative. Haman is the arch villain in Esther's story. He serves in a role not unlike prime minister and exudes all the vanity, arrogance, and self-importance of the title. Apparently, he is one of the king's favorites as well. Haman is of such prominence that Ahasuerus issues orders for all other government officials to bow in Haman's presence.

This was construed as a sign of public respect. Mordecai, however, viewed it as an insult.

Mordecai refuses to pay homage to Haman (Esth 3:2). Why? The reason for his refusal is not explained. This omission has led to a long debate with no definitive answer. The leading opinion seems to be that Mordecai was following the example of his ancestors. Generations earlier Shadrach, Meshach, and Abednego found themselves in a similar position. The great King Nebuchadnezzar constructed a golden image and demanded that everyone bow to it in worship (Dan 3). These three young men refused to comply out of their devotion to God.

Likewise, Daniel was cast into the den of lions because he disobeyed the law prohibiting prayer to any entity other than King Darius (Dan 6). Mordecai seems to be following this same trajectory, refusing to bow out of devotion to God.

This is a convenient interpretation, but not one well supported by the narrative. Remember, God's name is not even mentioned in this book. God is moving behind the scenes. We are forced to look for a different motivation for Mordecai's behavior, and we find it in the description of Mordecai's adversary, Haman.

The writer introduces Haman as the "son of Hammedatha the Agagite." The description is a bit vague, but it points to Haman being a descendent of King Agag the Amalekite (McConville, 166). This is the view of the Jewish historian Josephus as well (*Antiquities* 11.6.5). This Amalekite connection changes completely how one should read the events of Esther 3.

The Israelites and the Amalekites had a long, bitter history. When the nation of Israel was leaving Egypt under the leadership of Moses, the Amalekites attacked them shortly after they

> Consult the following for the generations-long hostility between the Amalekites and the Israelites:
>
> • Exodus 17:8-16: The Amalekites attack the newly liberated nation of Israel.
> • Numbers 24:20: The prophet Balaam condemns Amalek.
> • Deuteronomy 25:17-19: The destruction of the Amalekites is promised.
> • Judges 3:13; 6:3; 10:12: The Amalekites oppress Israel.
> • 1 Samuel 15: King Saul goes to war with King Agag.
> • Psalm 83:7: Asaph cries out for deliverance and vengeance against the Amalekites.

crossed the Red Sea (Exod 17:8–16), intentionally striking the old, the infirm, and those lagging behind. Centuries later, the Amalekite King Agag met the Israelite King Saul in battle (1 Sam 15). There Saul was commanded to avenge the injustices of the past. The loathing of the Israelites may best be summarized in a terrible promise recorded in Deuteronomy 25:17–19:

> Remember what Amalek did to you on your journey out of Egypt, how he attacked you on the way, when you were faint and weary, and struck down all who lagged behind you; he did not fear God. Therefore when the LORD your God has given you rest from all your enemies on every hand, in the land that the LORD your God is giving you as an inheritance to possess, you shall blot out the remembrance of Amalek from under heaven; do not forget.

Mordecai, though far from his homeland, is not far from his heritage. He has not forgotten the injustices of the past. No self-respecting Jew was ever going to bow before an Amalekite. And while this is some 500 years after the Benjaminite Saul went to battle against Agag, the Benjaminite Mordecai is still at war.

While Haman is narcissistic, needing celebrity and the accolades of others, more than jealousy drives the story of Esther. The conflict between Haman and Mordecai is not merely personal; it is a racially charged confrontation between historical enemies. This is the only viable explanation as to why Mordecai will not bow before Haman, and why Haman chooses to do more than take only Mordecai's life. Haman, in hatching a genocidal plot against the entire Jewish nation, is attempting to complete the work begun by his ancestors generations earlier.

Mordecai is a good and just man, but to interpret his actions as simple faithfulness is to overreach. Mordecai's action, coupled with Haman's reaction, now puts the entire Jewish populace in jeopardy.

Understanding

Confrontations are inevitable. Sometimes these confrontations are personal, involving a spouse, child, or parent. We know these all too well. Other confrontations ignite at work, on the ball field, in the boardroom, or even in the church sanctuary. Potential disagreements and misunderstandings are as numerous as the people in our lives. All relationships, no matter their depth, are prone to conflict. This isn't a pessimistic assessment; it is the nature of being human.

All of us are complex mixtures of our past, our education, our experiences, our beliefs, and our upbringing. It is impossible to divorce ourselves of these things, for they have made us who we are, good or bad. Our challenge is to recognize how this combination of environment and temperament has shaped us and the people around us. Often the most heated differences between people are produced by a failure to appreciate those differences and by a failure to understand where others are coming from.

Still, working as diligently as we can to understand others, we will be misunderstood. Our efforts to ensure justice will be misinterpreted as hardness of heart. Our attempts to be fair for all will be accepted as favoritism for some and prejudice against others. Our very existence—based on our gender, race, nationality, or political or religious affiliation—will be grounds enough for some to draw prejudiced conclusions about who we really are.

How do we control the reactions of others? We can't. Certainly when we act in an inappropriate or inflammatory way we may have to face the consequences of our actions. At other times, even when understanding, fairness, and kindness have been our trademark, we will still have to face the antagonistic reaction of others.

What About Me?

• *We are often the bearers of our forebears' battles and resentments.* At the time of Esther it had been some 500 years since the last war between the Israelites and the Amalekites. The original conflict was over 1,000 years in the past. Yet the hostility was still alive and well in Mordecai and Haman. Both were reaping the bitter harvest of history. At some point, someone has to stop the hostility by working toward resolution.

• *Rarely is one party in a conflict completely at fault and the other completely innocent.* It helps make sense of arguments by dividing those involved into camps designated "right" and "wrong." National, corporate, and individual conflicts are seldom that clear-cut. Confrontation is often complicated, multi-layered, and more nuanced than we recognize.

• *Personal battles often escalate to involve those around us.* At first, Mordecai and Haman's ill will toward one other appears to be personal, but it quickly expands into a genocidal plot to destroy the entire Jewish race. Mordecai may not have anticipated this move on Haman's part, but now he had to face it. Our personal skirmishes hardly ever stay contained to a single battlefield. They spin quickly out of control, involving those we care for deeply.

• *Past sticking points of prejudice or intolerance can scuttle our future.* The past Amalekite-Israeli conflict bore bitter fruit for both sides. In the book of Esther, that pattern continues. Our lives are no different. The conflicts and confrontations of our past can become the roadblocks that prevent us from moving into the future.

• *While we cannot control the reactions of others, we can do something about our own reactions.* Reconciliation is the task of all believers (2 Cor 5:19). This does not mean reconciliation will always be welcomed. The reactions of others are beyond our control. Our reaction in conflict with others, submissive to the Spirit, is our own responsibility.

Resources

Donald B. Kraybill, *The Upside-Down Kingdom, 25th Anniversary Edition* (Scottdale: Herald Press, 2003).

J. G. McConville, *The Daily Study Bible Series: Ezra, Nehemiah, and Esther* (Philadelphia: Westminster Press, 1985).

MORDECAI ANGERS HAMAN

Esther 3:1-15

Two Thumbs Down?

Every once in a while movie producers think there might be a profit in the book of Esther. In the 1960 film *Esther and the King*, Joan Collins played the part of Esther. In 2001's *Esther: A Veggie Tales Cartoon*, Esther was played by what appears to be a green onion, but could be a thin cucumber. For the 2007 big-screen version, the filmmakers had a twenty-million-dollar budget. They secured the talents of Peter O'Toole and Omar Sharif and used the leftover money on a young hunk to play the king, beautiful costumes, and extravagant set designs.

The critics were not kind to *One Night with the King*. They accused the filmmakers of stiff storytelling and bland dialogue. One review began,

> Dear Lord, why must your most ardent followers unleash such bad movies in your name? Surely, as our Creator, you wish for us to have better entertainment than the cut-rate fare that passes for faith-based film. Please hear the prayers of religious film producers, who are beseeching you for better scripts, larger budgets and bigger audiences. Surely Lord, moviegoers would be thankful if next time you inspired more talented people to take on one of your most beloved stories. (Josh Bell, "Dear Lord," *Las Vegas Weekly*, 12 October 2006)

It's hard to understand how they missed. The book of Esther offers sex, violence, and a dramatic subplot involving rivalry and revenge.

I. The Odd Couple

Mordecai and Haman were Cain and Abel, Ali and Frazier, Popeye and Bluto. They were born to hate one another.

After his cousin Esther became queen, Mordecai was "sitting at the king's gate" (2:21)—perhaps because Esther had arranged a job for him there. Esther followed Mordecai's advice to conceal her Jewish identity, but Mordecai wasn't nearly so careful. On this occasion, Mordecai was in the right place at the right time. Two guards wanted to kill the king. Bigthan and Teresh didn't know Mordecai was related to the first lady, so they revealed their plan to assassinate Ahasuerus. Mordecai told Esther, Esther told the king, and the king hanged the men who should have kept their mouths shut. The incident made it into the official history.

About the same time, the king promoted Haman to second in command. Ahasuerus decreed that everyone had to bow before his grand vizier. Haman adored this new position. He loved signing his name to important documents, loved knowing that people were trying not to stare, and particularly loved the bowing and kneeling. And one guy drove him crazy.

When the vizier came prancing by, Mordecai refused to grovel in the dust like everybody else. Mordecai wasn't impressed with VIPs, didn't care for celebrities, and wouldn't bow to any bigwig. When Haman's people asked Mordecai why he was disrespecting their boss, Mordecai said he was a Jew. They spoke to Mordecai about it several times, but he continued to be disagreeable. Finally they went to Haman to see if he could do something about Mordecai.

Revealing Mordecai's Jewishness didn't help matters with Haman, who was a raging anti-Semite. At first he thought about taking out his anger directly on Mordecai, but then decided he needed to do more. He believed that not only was Mordecai disagreeable; *all* Jews were disagreeable. Twenty-four centuries before Hitler, Haman had his own "final solution." Haman had the *pur*—the lot—cast to pick the day on which to exterminate the Jews.

Haman set a trap by appealing to the king's vanity: "Your majesty, you have some subjects who aren't loyal. I am, however, such a loyal subject that I don't want you to have to put up with such insolence. Persia is crawling with these odd people. They don't fit in; their ways are different from everybody else's. It's obvious they don't care for the king. They disregard your laws. The only thing to do is exterminate all of them. If it would make you happy, just give the word and they'll be destroyed. I'll not only take care of all the expense, but I'll also donate several wheelbarrows full of silver to the treasury for the privilege."

Without thinking much about it, the king went along with the plan. They scheduled the destruction of the Jews. The lawyers wrote it up, and an edict was proclaimed throughout the kingdom. Bulletins were sent everywhere ordering the massacre of all Jews—men, women, and children—on a single day.

Esther 3:15 offers a telling detail. The text doesn't mention Ahasuerus bothering to find out why Haman hated the Jews or even learning the identity of the people whose death warrant he agreed to sign. Then we read, "The king and Haman sat down to drink, but the city of Susa was bewildered." The partners in crime sit in rocking chairs on the porch toasting their vicious scheme with another beer, while ordinary people reel from the horrific news.

II. An Empty Emperor

When called by the more common version of his name, Xerxes is the only person in the Bible whose name begins with an X. There's not much else we can say for him. Ahasuerus was a buffoon, a hothead, and a showoff. We want to like Ahasuerus because he's married to the heroine, but the book of Esther portrays him as lazy, self-indulgent, and immoral. The contemporary Greek historian Herodotus backs up this assessment (Colin Sedgwick, "God Is Working His Purpose Out," *Expository Times* 114 [2003]: 381–82).

The king would have been seen as a tragic-comic figure by the first readers of Esther because of his decadent tastes and propensity for writing unrealistic laws in the middle of parties. Ahasuerus's empire lived under the rule of a clown who could not control his own wife and appeared helpless to act without the advice of his counselors.

Xerxes reminds us to pay attention to our moral responsibilities and not to yield to our laziness.

III. A Despicable Despot

Haman was unspeakably evil. He surrendered his soul to hatred of his rival Mordecai. He misled the king to carry out his plan for genocide. Ethnic cleansing is, sadly, not a new idea.

Haman told the king that the Jewish laws were enough motivation for the people's destruction. The Jews' speech, diet, dress, and religious customs were different from those of Persia. Haman hated Mordecai and the Jews because their religious convictions made them a separate people.

Our flaws may not be as obvious as Haman's, but we are tempted by jealousy and ambition. Why wasn't Haman satisfied by his level of success? Why aren't we? Why was Haman so bothered by the mere presence of his rival? Why are we? The poison that destroyed Haman is still a threat.

IV. An Obstinate Opponent

Mordecai is a loving yet headstrong person. The writer doesn't explain his decision not to kneel before Haman. Mordecai may have refused to bow to the emperor's new vizier because Haman was an Agagite (3:1-2). A sworn enmity existed between the people of Amalek and Israel dating back to the time of the exodus (Exod 17:16). King Saul fought against King Agag and the Amalekites (1 Sam 15:2). Mordecai may have refused to bow to Haman, the descendant of Agag, because such a gesture of respect to an old enemy was too much for him. The most positive interpretation is that Mordecai's refusal to bow to this enemy of God's people is evidence that he considered himself a citizen of God's kingdom first, and only secondarily a citizen of Ahasuerus's empire. A more skeptical explanation is that Mordecai's action was based on his view that a person with Haman's background did not deserve respect (Iain Duguid, "The Eschatology of the Book of Esther," *Westminster Theological Journal* 68 [2006]: 86–90).

Was it wise for Mordecai not to bow before Haman? The hard truth is that the Jews' deadly predicament was a direct result of Mordecai's refusal to bow.

V. Picking Our Fights

How do we know when to start an argument? How long do we let disagreements last? How do we respond to others' negative reactions?

We can imagine what Mordecai and Haman felt for one another. Some of our competitors don't give us the respect we think we've earned, racist neighbors think they're better than anyone else, and members of our Sunday school class take the best donuts. When the phone rings, we hope some people *aren't* on the other end. When we go to a party, we hope certain individuals didn't get invited.

We don't love some people the least little bit—the in-laws who forever mess up their own lives and complicate ours in the process, the boss who keeps turning down a long overdue raise, and the know-it-all who dismisses our ideas. Is there someone who makes you wince just by being present?

We don't want to love our enemies. They make us feel superior. Jonathan Swift said, "We have just enough religion to make us hate, but not enough to make us love."

We aren't often involved in life-and-death disputes, but we know our way around animosity. Someone at work says something mean that gets back to you. Your choices seem limited to challenging or ignoring them, but other possibilities exist. Say something good about them. Bless those who curse you.

An old friend always bores you with stories about how great she is. Your choices seem to be insulting her or being bored out of your mind. You could, however, tell your own story about her greatness. That will confuse her. Bless those who annoy you.

Your spouse breaks a promise. Your choices seem to be confronting your partner or acting like you've chosen to overlook it. You could, however, cover up the mistake so the person never knows that you know. Bless those who fail you.

VI. A Different Ending

What would have happened if Mordecai and Haman had taken the time to listen to one another? Imagine Dr. Phil saying, "Mordecai, tell Haman what you feel when your relatives are forced to bow down before him. Haman, tell Mordecai what you feel when he disrespects the king's second-in-command."

Did Haman ever ask himself what it means to be a Jew? Did Mordecai ever wonder how a descendant of King Agag felt about King Saul slaughtering his ancestors?

We must strive to remember that someone else may consider us their enemies. How do we behave toward others? Are we the cruel ones, the annoying ones, or the unfaithful ones? What do we see when we look carefully at one another? If we look into the eyes of someone who despises us, we may understand the pain that makes them hate. If we look into the eyes of a victim of prejudice, we'll raise our voices against racism. If we look into the eyes of a boss who keeps taking bad advice and making bad decisions, we'll try to give them encouragement.

If we look into the eyes of a lonely person, we'll listen.

If we look into the eyes of a lost person, we'll tell them the story of Christ.

If we look into the eyes of an enemy, we may see a potential friend.

As with most situations in life, Jesus' golden rule applies: "Do to others as you would have them do to you" (Lk 6:31).

Notes

Notes

3

Mordecai Intercedes

Esther 4

Central Question

How can I help others through my position in life?

Scripture

Esther 4 1 When Mordecai learned all that had been done, Mordecai tore his clothes and put on sackcloth and ashes, and went through the city, wailing with a loud and bitter cry; 2 he went up to the entrance of the king's gate, for no one might enter the king's gate clothed with sackcloth. 3 In every province, wherever the king's command and his decree came, there was great mourning among the Jews, with fasting and weeping and lamenting, and most of them lay in sackcloth and ashes. 4 When Esther's maids and her eunuchs came and told her, the queen was deeply distressed; she sent garments to clothe Mordecai, so that he might take off his sackcloth; but he would not accept them. 5 Then Esther called for Hathach, one of the king's eunuchs, who had been appointed to attend her, and ordered him to go to Mordecai to learn what was happening and why. 6 Hathach went out to Mordecai in the open square of the city in front of the king's gate, 7 and Mordecai told him all that had happened to him, and the exact sum of money that Haman had promised to pay into the king's treasuries for the destruction of the Jews. 8 Mordecai also gave him a copy of the written decree issued in Susa for their destruction, that he might show it to Esther, explain it to her, and charge her to go to the king to make supplication to him and entreat him for her people. 9 Hathach went and told

Esther what Mordecai had said. 10 Then Esther spoke to Hathach and gave him a message for Mordecai, saying, 11 "All the king's servants and the people of the king's provinces know that if any man or woman goes to the king inside the inner court without being called, there is but one law—all alike are to be put to death. Only if the king holds out the golden scepter to someone, may that person live. I myself have not been called to come in to the king for thirty days." 12 When they told Mordecai what Esther had said, 13 Mordecai told them to reply to Esther, "Do not think that in the king's palace you will escape any more than all the other Jews. 14 For if you keep silence at such a time as this, relief and deliverance will rise for the Jews from another quarter, but you and your father's family will perish. Who knows? Perhaps you have come to royal dignity for just such a time as this." 15 Then Esther said in reply to Mordecai, 16 "Go, gather all the Jews to be found in Susa, and hold a fast on my behalf, and neither eat nor drink for three days, night or day. I and my maids will also fast as you do. After that I will go to the king, though it is against the law; and if I perish, I perish." 17 Mordecai then went away and did everything as Esther had ordered him.

Reflecting

Mount Pinatubo erupted in the Philippines in the summer of 1991. More than 200 people were killed and 200,000 displaced. One group, the Aetas, were especially devastated by the eruption. The Aeta tribe is a group of aboriginal people who live on the slopes of Mount Pinatubo. For them, Pinatubo is a place of destiny. They feel they have no choice but to call this dangerous place home.

After the eruption, the Filipino government planned to build new settlements and relocate the Aetas. This was refused. Against the instructions of Western geologists and Filipino authorities, the tribe returned to their homes on Pinatubo. The Aetas are ruled by doom. They have concluded that fate dictates their future. Pinatubo is not merely a place they call home. It is the only place where they feel they are ordained to live.

This kind of fatalism once played a prominent role in American life as well. One factor identified in the high rate of past tornado fatalities in the South's Bible Belt was the people's belief that all events are inevitable and they should submit to their fate.

Upon hearing a tornado warning, those in the Midwest, Great Plains, and other portions of the country would respond with action. They would seek shelter, go to the basement, or get out of the path of the storm. Southerners, steeped in a kind of Christian fatalism, tended to understand the threat as an inescapable act of God. They saw themselves as powerless to act. They huddled in their clapboard houses and prayed for deliverance.

While this type of fatalism has eroded, many people still maintain a blind fatalism in their personal lives. When the world collapses around them, they resign themselves to a life of misery, waiting for the other shoe to drop. They give up, feeling powerless to do anything (McBrayer, 41).

Studying

Chapter 4 is an important transition in Esther's story, a hinge upon which the book turns. Chapter 4 is also home to the most familiar verses from the book. In verse 14 Mordecai tells Esther that her rise to royalty may possibly be "for just such a time as this." Her becoming queen has been the result of more than beauty, sex appeal, and spa treatments. God has brought her life to this crossroads to save the Jewish nation from destruction.

Esther's response, "If I perish, I perish" (v. 16), is also noteworthy. It is not the response of one who has given up, waving the white flag of surrender. It is a response of courage, determination, and resolve in the face of an indefinite outcome.

As Haman's plans to exterminate the Jews ripples through the Persian Empire, the result is predictable and expected. Jewish communities, already made vulnerable by past deportations and apparent widespread anti-Semitism, erupt in mourning. Fasting, weeping, the customary tearing of outer clothing, and the donning of sackcloth and ashes are widespread. The entire nation mourns in distress. Mordecai puts on the garments of sorrow and begins a parade through the streets of Susa.

Clothed in the traditional dress of mourning, Mordecai walks toward the king's palace to get Esther's attention. It works. She quickly sends proper clothes for him to wear and inquires as to the reason for his behavior. Maybe she thought there had been a death in the family or a personal crisis of some kind. She probably never dreamed of hearing the terrible news delivered to her—that the entire Jewish nation was in peril.

Esther's position as queen insulated her from the outside world. Her status kept her literally in an ivory tower. Indeed, in our story Esther is so insulated that she is completely unaware of her people's predicament and the plot against them. The imminent destruction of her nation is news to her. Even living at the heart of the empire, in the same building as the king, she is oblivious to the danger.

> Dressing in sackcloth and ashes is a custom of intense mourning found repeatedly in the Old Testament. It appears as early as Genesis 37 as the patriarch Jacob mourned over the supposed death of his son Joseph. It is a favorite phrase found in the Psalms and the Prophets as an outward sign of a broken heart and repentance. Sackcloth was exactly that: course material, usually of camel or goat hair, used to make grain sacks. Worn on the body, it was rough, scratchy, and uncomfortable, an appropriate way of communicating how the mourner actually felt. The ashes sprinkled on top of the head or rubbed on the face produced dark stains, an ancient way of showing the black clouds of grief hanging over a person's head.

Yet Mordecai is quick to point out that this danger is dreadfully real, even to Esther. There is a reason, if not an obligation, for Esther to use her position to intervene "for just such a time as this." If she is not motivated to save her nation, at least she might be motivated to save herself.

While Esther's position as queen had prevented her from hearing the horrible news about a looming genocide, this same position would not protect her from being destroyed. Rank-and-file Jews might escape the coming disaster. They could run, hide, or disguise their identity just as Esther had done. But if her identity were discovered—a Jew married to the king and living in the palace—Esther would not escape. If Haman gained this informa-

tion first, he would likely spin it in such a way as to make her look like a conspirator in some great plot to harm the king. Israel was in danger, but so was Esther.

There was a silver lining, however, to Mordecai's dark cloud. The conspirator Haman was a powerful politician, maybe the most powerful man in the kingdom besides King Ahasuerus. Yet there was one other person who had a place of unparalleled position and power: Esther. As queen, if she played her hand wisely by striking first, she held the political trump card. Mordecai knew this and implored her to use it.

There was only one problem: an ambiguous Persian law did not allow impromptu visits to the king. The Persian king was like any national leader. For the sake of security he was kept in isolation, his movements and schedule dictated by strict rules of command and control. To approach him without being summoned was to risk death. This security practice sheltered the king from unwarranted danger.

It was therefore a deadly proposition for Esther to enter the king's presence without an appointment or summons. Her situation was made even more precarious by the fact that this king wasn't afraid to remove a queen for minor violations (see Esth 1).

Esther, who enjoyed a charmed life and had much to lose, decided to intervene. She sent word back to Mordecai to this effect. She asked her people to fast on her behalf as she prepared herself to enter the king's presence.

In the most explicit reference to God in the book of Esther, Mordecai reveals his trust in providence. In verse 14 he tells Esther, "For if you keep silence at such a time as this, relief and deliverance will rise for the Jews from another quarter." Recall that Haman was an Agagite, a descendent of King Agag of the Amalekites. Mordecai held tightly to God's promise in Exodus 17:14 and Deuteronomy 25:17-19 that the Amalekites would one day be devastated by the Jewish nation for past crimes. This promise could not be fulfilled if Haman's plot succeeded.

As we find everywhere in the book of Esther, this is a subversive but clear trust in Yahweh as deliverer of the Jewish people. Mordecai believes that a God-directed escape will emerge, even if Esther refuses to intervene or falls short in her effort.

Understanding

The drama that is the book of Esther twists and turns on small acts that seem insignificant. Yet when these small acts are strung together, they shape the story of redemption. While God's name and overt actions are absent from the story, God is quietly at work in the modest actions of God's people. The book of Esther teaches us that we can follow this understated example. Our actions on behalf of others do not have to be larger than life. God's intentions can be accomplished even through the little things we do.

Consider Mordecai. His small act of public mourning with his sackcloth, sprinkled ashes, and pacing in front of the palace gained Esther's attention. Had he not done this, she would have continued living in ignorance of what was about to happen to her people. While the book bears her name and she is certainly a profile of courage, there would be no heroic Esther without Mordecai's simple actions. He was the only one who could reach her.

Further, notice that through a single conversation, Mordecai challenged Esther to intervene on behalf of others. His few words, carried to her by courier, changed the course of a nation. Once awakened to the dangers, Esther responded bravely and quickly, but she needed Mordecai to open her eyes and stir her courage. Again, only Mordecai, her cousin and adoptive father, could have this kind of influence on her.

Finally, it was Esther who made the decision to enter King Ahasuerus's throne room. It was an act only she could carry out. It was her time. She was uniquely positioned to bring about the survival of an entire people through one brave act. None of us have the ability to save the world single-handedly, but we can all do what we can where we have the opportunity. When our small acts come together with the countless small acts of others and God's power and purpose, truly outstanding things can be accomplished.

What is one thing you can do to serve others at this point and time in your life?

What About Me?

• *How have I been uniquely gifted or positioned to help others?* Religious superstars and professional clergy are not the only ones gifted for service in the kingdom of God. We all have God-given talents to use in spiritual service. Additionally, all people have distinct positions of service. How can your vocation or role in the community help others benefit from what only you can do?

• *Do I heed the good counsel of those God has put into my life?* Where would we be without wise people who have the courage to tell us the truth? A friend, a grandparent, a mentor or teacher: these people have the ability to look into our lives, see what is possible, and challenge us to do it. To discount or ignore their contribution to our lives is to miss out on fulfilling a much greater purpose.

• *Have I ever protected my own interests over the interests of those who truly need help?* It is human nature to protect our own well-being, but sometimes our self-interests are in conflict with the greater good. No one can serve others without putting aside their own priorities. Jesus said it best: "whoever wishes to be great among you must be your servant, and whoever wishes to be first among you must be your slave; just as the Son of Man came not to be served but to serve" (Mt 20:26–28).

• *Am I at an important crossroads in my life, requiring counsel, prayer, and courage?* As Esther prepared to enter King Ahasuerus's presence, she pleaded for her people to fast on her behalf that her resolve would not fail. When we come to major decisions in life, we need the same things as Esther: faithful counsel from the wise, prayer, fasting, and courage to do the right thing even in the face of an uncertain outcome.

Resource

Ronnie McBrayer, *But God Meant It for God: Lessons from the Life of Joseph* (Macon GA: Smyth and Helwys, 2007).

MORDECAI
INTERCEDES
Esther 4

Righteous Women

A courageous woman saves Jews from extermination at great risk to her own life. It could be the fifth century bc or it could be the 1940s. Ona Simaite was a librarian at the University of Vilna in Lithuania. She convinced the Germans that she needed to collect library books from students in the Jewish ghetto. She used this excuse to deliver bread, jam, and cheese to children in the orphanage. Simaite ran errands and smuggled in false papers. She attended ghetto cultural events as a sign of her solidarity with the persecuted. She saved dozens of children by smuggling them out and finding homes for them. On one occasion she saved a young girl from a mob. Her help of the Jews didn't go unnoticed. Simaite was sent to Dachau and tortured. She survived and later said of the war years, "Those were the happiest days of my life" (David Gushee, *The Righteous Gentiles of the Holocaust* [Minneapolis: Fortress, 1994] 85–86).

It would be interesting to know how Esther felt years later as she remembered the conflict with Haman.

I. The Threat

When they learned of the edict that announced their execution, the Jews in Persia began to mourn. Before Esther knew what was going on, she heard that Mordecai was outside the gate wearing sackcloth. She did not want her cousin to draw attention to himself, so she sent out fresh clothes.

When Mordecai returned the clothing, she realized there was a problem. Her messenger got the whole story from Mordecai. Haman had pressed the king to create the edict, and then he had financed the massacre of the Jews. Mordecai even sent a copy of the decree ordering the slaughter. He had the servant tell Esther to go to the king and plead for her people.

When Esther received the message, she was frightened and sent back a reasonable excuse: "There's nothing I can do. The king is notoriously moody. Everyone who works in the palace knows that if you approach the king without being invited you can be executed. You have to hope that he extends his gold scepter or you die. Things aren't going so well with my husband. We haven't spoken in a month. This isn't a chance I can take. It's too dangerous. I have to stay out of this. There's nothing I can do."

Mordecai was not sympathetic. He sent a cryptic response: "What makes you believe you will be safe? Don't think that you will be the one Jew who lives through this. 'Kill all the Jews' means 'all the Jews'—and that means you, too. Maybe you became queen for just such a time as this."

II. The Question

The best known verse in Esther is Mordecai's attempt to persuade the queen to take her life into her hands and influence the king. Mordecai's response is usually translated, "For if you keep silence at such a time as this, relief and deliverance will rise for the Jews from another quarter, but you and your father's family will perish. Who knows? Perhaps you have come to royal dignity for just such a time as this."

Esther 4:14 is essentially the center of the story. It reads like a thinly veiled reference to God's providence working behind the scenes. Since Esther contains no direct references to God, this verse becomes even more significant.

Up to this point in the story, Esther has taken no initiative. In this verse, Mordecai seems to say that if Esther doesn't do anything to help the Jews, they will still be saved. Even more surprising is the idea that if she doesn't act, she and her family will be killed.

Does this make sense? How might the Jews be delivered without Esther's help? Some suggest that the phrase "another quarter" is actually a substitute for God. The difficulty with this interpretation is the word "another." "Another God" makes no sense. The author also deliberately keeps God out of the spotlight throughout the story.

It is possible that Mordecai hoped other Jews holding high offices would act, that the Jews would rise up in revolt, or that sympathetic Persians would intervene. Maybe another country would attack. None of these guesses seem likely. The story never hints at other possibilities.

It's also hard to understand why, if relief came from another quarter, Esther and her family would still be killed. Would God punish Esther for not standing up for her people? Was Mordecai trying to convince Esther that the Jews would consider her a traitor? If so, why did he direct the threat at Esther's "father's family"? Her father's family was Mordecai's family. Mordecai was an older cousin who raised the orphan Esther as his own daughter. Why would God's judgment or Jewish vengeance fall on Mordecai's family?

One scholar argues that the most accurate translation of Esther 4:14 is, "For if you certainly keep silent at this time, *will* relief and deliverance arise for the Jews from another place? Then you and the house of your father will be destroyed."

If this translation is correct, then Mordecai is saying that Esther is the only possible source of relief and deliverance for the Jews (John M. Wiebe, "Will Relief and Deliverance Arise for the Jews from Another Place?" *The Catholic Biblical Quarterly* 53 [1991]: 409–15).

III. The Danger

We've heard the story of Esther so often that we forget it might have turned out differently. God's people aren't always courageous.

In 1994, 800,000 people were murdered in 100 days in Rwanda, a small African country where two-thirds of the people are Christian. Fleeing from genocide, ethnic Tutsis sought safety in churches. Rather than serving as sanctuaries, the churches became slaughterhouses. One of the most chilling accounts took place at a Christian camp in Mugonero, where Tutsis, including seven pastors, had gathered. Upon hearing of an impending massacre, the pastors asked church president Elizaphan Ntakirutimana, an ethnic Hutu and a community leader, for help. They wrote, "We have heard that tomorrow we will be killed with our families, and we ask you in the name of the Lord to intercede on our behalf, just as Esther saved the Jews."

Not only did Ntakirutimana choose not to help, but he presided over the mass murder at the camp. He was later arrested in Laredo, Texas, and was eventually extradited to Rwanda. Again and again, Rwandan Christians failed their communities in a time of crisis ("Courageous Churches," http://www.acaciaresources.com).

Between courageous Christians and evil hypocrites are many indifferent people. They do little harm and show little faith. Some who call themselves Christians care too little, take few risks, and pay scant attention to the world's suffering because it's still dangerous to try to save the persecuted.

IV. The Response

Esther decided to risk a trip to the gas chamber. She sent back her answer: "Get all of the Jews together. Tell them to fast and I'll do the same. If you do this, I'll go to the king, even though it's forbidden. If I die, I die."

Esther was raised as an Israelite. As a child, she learned the stories of Yahweh, the King whose riches cannot be measured in silver and gold, whose power isn't in horses and chariots. Though she was now surrounded by the comforts and luxuries of a palace, she also held the hopes of her people. Esther's story makes us ask, "How can we help others through our position in life?"

Of all the horrific scenes in *Schindler's List*, the most painful may be the last. The Jews rescued by this righteous Gentile named Oskar Schindler express their gratitude for his help. They tell him how thankful they are for the risks he took and the financial expenditures he made to save them from the gas chambers.

As they express their appreciation, he begins to weep and says, "I could have done so much more!" He points to his expensive car and says, "See that car? I could have sold it and used the money to save the lives of several others." Over and over he says, "I could have done so much more. I could have done so much more."

We can do so much more. Most of the time, our choices don't seem to be matters of great significance, but they can still affect the people around us who need help. The painful truth is that we have the ability to make a difference for all kinds of people. We can help God save the hungry, lonely, and lost.

V. The Sunday School

The class always begins by sharing prayer concerns. Most of the time it's routine—a cousin who is having a knee operation, a possible promotion at work. Then one Sunday someone says something unexpected: "Six months ago, I took painkillers after my surgery. I haven't been able to stop taking them, and I don't want to stop, but I need to pray to stop."

The room becomes quiet. No one is sure how to respond. Then a woman who seldom speaks says, "My husband died five years ago and people don't talk about him anymore. I've started to forget things about him that I used to know, and it makes me cry. You're not supposed to be crying five years after someone dies."

After more silence, a father speaks: "I'm always talking about how well my son is doing. This week he got drunk and wrecked his car. Now I realize he's had a drinking problem for some time. I don't know how to make him understand how serious this is."

The woman seated next to him says, "Thank you for saying what you're really praying for and not just what sounds like a prayer request. I've been thinking about prayer this week and I've decided I've been missing a lot. I'm always praying for my sick friends, my family, my problems. That can't be enough. Shouldn't we pray about the problems in the world?"

Taken aback, the teacher asks a question that isn't in her notes: "Whom should we be worried about? What should we be praying about?"

"We need to pray for the earth. We're not leaving it in good shape for our grandchildren."

"We need to pray for Christians around the world. The church is too timid."

"We need to pray for people who are lonely. It's hard to be by yourself."

"We need to pray about hunger. When I hear the statistics—25,000 people a day dying—the numbers are so overwhelming that I don't want to believe it's true, because then I'd have to do something."

"I'm afraid I've stopped praying about war. I'm overwhelmed by how many people die. I don't know how to pray about numbers that big. I can't keep straight who's killing who, but I should keep praying about it."

Could it be that the prayer concerns God places on our hearts echo Mordecai's urging that we serve "in such a time as this"?

Notes

Notes

4

ESTHER
TAKES A RISK

Esther 5:1-8; 7:1–8:2

Central Question

What risk is God calling me to take?

Scripture

Esther 5:1-8; 7:1–8:2 5:1 On the third day Esther put on her royal robes and stood in the inner court of the king's palace, opposite the king's hall. The king was sitting on his royal throne inside the palace opposite the entrance to the palace. 2 As soon as the king saw Queen Esther standing in the court, she won his favor and he held out to her the golden scepter that was in his hand. Then Esther approached and touched the top of the scepter. 3 The king said to her, "What is it, Queen Esther? What is your request? It shall be given you, even to the half of my kingdom." 4 Then Esther said, "If it pleases the king, let the king and Haman come today to a banquet that I have prepared for the king." 5 Then the king said, "Bring Haman quickly, so that we may do as Esther desires." So the king and Haman came to the banquet that Esther had prepared. 6 While they were drinking wine, the king said to Esther, "What is your petition? It shall be granted you. And what is your request? Even to the half of my kingdom, it shall be fulfilled." 7 Then Esther said, "This is my petition and request: 8 If I have won the king's favor, and if it pleases the king to grant my petition and fulfill my request, let the king and Haman come tomorrow to the banquet that I will prepare for them, and then I will do as the king has said."…. 7:1 So the king and Haman went in to feast with Queen Esther.

2 On the second day, as they were drinking wine, the king again said to Esther, "What is your petition, Queen Esther? It shall be granted you. And what is your request? Even to the half of my kingdom, it shall be fulfilled." 3 Then Queen Esther answered, "If I have won your favor, O king, and if it pleases the king, let my life be given me—that is my petition—and the lives of my people—that is my request. 4 For we have been sold, I and my people, to be destroyed, to be killed, and to be annihilated. If we had been sold merely as slaves, men and women, I would have held my peace; but no enemy can compensate for this damage to the king." 5 Then King Ahasuerus said to Queen Esther, "Who is he, and where is he, who has presumed to do this?" 6 Esther said, "A foe and enemy, this wicked Haman!" Then Haman was terrified before the king and the queen. 7 The king rose from the feast in wrath and went into the palace garden, but Haman stayed to beg his life from Queen Esther, for he saw that the king had determined to destroy him. 8 When the king returned from the palace garden to the banquet hall, Haman had thrown himself on the couch where Esther was reclining; and the king said, "Will he even assault the queen in my presence, in my own house?" As the words left the mouth of the king, they covered Haman's face. 9 Then Harbona, one of the eunuchs in attendance on the king, said, "Look, the very gallows that Haman has prepared for Mordecai, whose word saved the king, stands at Haman's house, fifty cubits high." And the king said, "Hang him on that." 10 So they hanged Haman on the gallows that he had prepared for Mordecai. Then the anger of the king abated. 8:1 On that day King Ahasuerus gave to Queen Esther the house of Haman, the enemy of the Jews; and Mordecai came before the king, for Esther had told what he was to her. 2 Then the king took off his signet ring, which he had taken from Haman, and gave it to Mordecai. So Esther set Mordecai over the house of Haman.

Reflecting

January 13, 1982, was a cold, snowy day in the nation's capital. A massive blizzard delayed the travel of commuters trying to get home from work and air travelers trying to leave the city. At the height of the storm, Air Florida Flight 90 took off from Washington D.C.'s National Airport. After just minutes in the air, it struck the 14th Street Bridge and plunged into the icy waters of the Potomac River.

Hundreds of onlookers gathered on the damaged bridge and the snow-covered banks of the river to watch the rescue attempt of the precious few survivors. One man, twenty-eight-year-old Lenny Skutnik, quickly went from being an observer to a participant in a daring act of courage.

Skutnik was an assistant in the Congressional Budget office making less than $20,000 a year. He had a simple life with his wife and two young sons. He had never taken a life-saving or first aid course. Paying his $325 monthly rent was his biggest regular challenge. Yet when he saw a woman blinded by shock and jet fuel, too weak to grasp the rings being lowered by a rescue helicopter, Lenny went into the freezing water after her.

Later that month, President Ronald Reagan seated Lenny Skutnik in the chambers of the U.S. Congress as his guest for the State of the Union address. Reagan said, "Nothing had picked him out particularly to be a hero, but without hesitation there he was and he saved her life."

> When have you been in a position to take a risk for the good of someone else? What did you do? Why? Do you ever regret your decision?

Skutnik resisted all efforts to make his risky act into something heroic. He said, "Nobody else was doing anything. It was the only way.... I just did it" (Bennett, 505–07).

Studying

As the drama of chapter 5 unfolds, we find Esther standing outside the king's private hall, unannounced and unsummoned, preparing to enter. The future of the Jewish people, not to mention her own future, hinges on the risky act of Esther entering Ahasuerus's throne room. She knew that entering a Persian king's presence without appointment was to put her life in danger. Only the extension of the royal scepter, a symbol of approval and welcome, could signal mercy and spare the individual from certain death.

It turns out that Esther has nothing to fear; Ahasuerus finds her irresistible. Knowing her visit is for some important purpose, he extends his scepter, invites her in, and offers up to half his kingdom to satisfy her request. It is a blank check, but not one she is yet willing to cash. Instead, she invites the king and Haman to a surprise banquet. Ahasuerus sends for Haman right away. They attend, and the king inquires again regarding Esther's request. Again, she delays, inviting Ahasuerus and Haman to a second feast to be held the following day.

Why would Esther delay in making her appeal? It is impossible to say. It is likely, however, that the author of the book is using a literary device to keep the reader in suspense. This is the author's way of flashing "To Be Continued..." across the screen, postponing the finale until the tension is unbearable.

Haman leaves Esther's first banquet in "good spirits" (Esth 5:9). He has just dined with the king at the request of the queen, the honored guest at a royal banquet. On his way home, he crosses paths with Mordecai, who refuses once again to bow and show honor to Haman. Enraged beyond reason and incited by his wife and friends, Haman builds a tall gallows upon which he plans to hang Mordecai for his disrespect (Esth 5:14). The planned genocide, still months in the future, is not happening soon enough for him. Haman plans a preemptive strike against Mordecai.

Even as the gallows is being built, the king has a restless night of sleep. To pass the night he has the book of records read aloud to him. Listening, he discovers that Mordecai once foiled an assassination attempt on his life, a heroic deed that went unrewarded:

> It was found written how Mordecai had told about Bigthana and Teresh, two of the king's eunuchs, who guarded the threshold, and who had conspired to assassinate King Ahasuerus. Then the king said, "What honor or distinction has been bestowed on Mordecai for this?" The king's servants who attended him said, "Nothing has been done for him." (Esth 6:1-3)

As Ahasuerus contemplates a reward, Haman enters the king's court. The king asks, "What shall be done for the man whom the king wishes to honor?" (Esth 6:6). In his arrogance, Haman thinks this honor will fall upon him. He details an elaborate display of recognition, but is much chagrined when his plan for self-commendation falls on Mordecai instead. In fact, Haman is ordered to escort Mordecai through the streets of Susa singing his praises. Haman returns home in humiliation, but before he can lick his wounds, he is summoned back to the palace for Esther's second banquet.

Finally, the story reaches its resolution. As the three sit down to eat, the king asks a third time what Esther desires; this time she asks for her life to be spared—a shocking and confusing revelation for her dinner guests. She points to Haman as the arch villain of her people, the very one who had misled the king into signing a genocidal edict against the Jews. Ahasuerus is enraged. He leaves the table, stepping out into the palace gardens. It is likely that his furious stroll through the gardens was to clear his head, to take in and process the new information, and to address his own foolishness for being easily duped by Haman, a man who had put the queen's life in jeopardy.

When Ahasuerus left Esther's banquet in anger, he did what Persian kings were fond of doing: he took a walk in his private garden. The Greek word for "paradise" seems to come from an Old Persian word for "enclosed" or "walled garden." These were personal paradises, so beautiful and peaceful that the word was adopted by other cultures to describe life after death.

In the king's absence, Haman throws himself, quite literally, on Esther's mercy. The Persian custom would have been to recline while eating. As Haman begs for his life, he falls onto Esther. The king returns at that precise moment, interpreting Haman's actions as a physical or sexual assault. Haman is condemned to death and is soon hung from the gallows intended for Mordecai.

Understanding

The end result of Esther's well-timed strategy is that Mordecai receives all the good originally intended for Haman, and Haman meets a fate intended for Mordecai. With Esther's prompting, Mordecai takes Haman's place in the king's court and inherits Haman's estate. The author's purpose is clear: God's providence has turned the destruction of the Jewish people back on their enemies. Yet God's hand did not move alone. Esther's risk-taking courage put these redemptive actions in motion.

One of the more mysterious aspects of Christian faith is the relationship between an all-powerful God and an all-too-limited humanity. How much does God control about the future, and how much is left for us to shape? Where does God's influence over circumstances end, to be replaced by our participation? Are we mere puppets on a string, playing out our part in a divine game? Is God even involved in our world, or is its fate simply up to us? There are no easy answers to these long-debated questions.

> You can live on bland food so as to avoid an ulcer; drink no tea or coffee or other stimulants, in the name of health; go to bed early and stay away from night life; avoid all controversial subjects...spend money only on necessities.... Still you [could fall and] break your neck in the bathtub, and it will serve you right.
> —Tim Hansel

Regardless of our conclusions, the book of Esther presents a God who has chosen to work through people rather than through mighty acts of divine power. This appears to be intentional restraint; God acts within a framework of self-imposed limitations. God refuses to operate independently of people who bravely answer the call of faith. God must be credited for conducting the beautiful symphony of life, but God will not play the music; that is left to people like Esther—like you and me. It seems that God is willing to live with the consequences of our failures or successes, secure in the fact that the divine purpose will still be accomplished.

> In what ways is Esther extraordinary? In what ways is she ordinary?

What About Me?

• *Where need and opportunity meet ability and compassion, God calls people of faith to act.* How do you know God wants you to do something? God is speaking where the needs of the world cross paths with your ability to meet those needs. Such opportunities cannot be ignored. We must heed them as the voice of God.

• *Explaining the details of how God works is not the goal of the Christian life.* For too long, believers have systemized and analyzed the characteristics of God until our explanations fit into neat packages or outlines. God is much larger than this, however, and much more mysterious. The connection between God's actions and our own is more like choreographed dancing than strict marching. It is not something we can explain. Rather, it is something in which we participate.

• *The life of faith is not the life of safety.* Our Lord did not lead a life of rationality and safety, nor did he call us to that path. Jesus didn't say, "Follow me and I will make you feel good.... Follow me and I will make you into a moral, upstanding citizen.... Follow me and I will make you impervious to doubt.... Follow me and I will make you trouble free." He said "Follow me, deny yourself, take up your cross, and take the risky path that leads to resurrection." This is not the way of playing it safe.

• *There are no superheroes who do God's work, only ordinary people.* Esther is in a long line of saints who were just plain normal. She was an average woman who found herself in an unexpected situation. Before becoming queen, she was an unremarkable Jewish girl far from home with only a distant relative to look after her. Yet God chooses to work with and through such individuals: ordinary people, like you and me, called to take extraordinary risks.

• *You never know what role your act of faith will play in the greater drama God is directing.* Esther's courage saved a nation. That courage is still celebrated thousands of years later. When you respond to God's call with courage and resolve, in spite of your fears, you enter into a series of events with unseen and unknown consequences. Those who live in future generations may reap the benefit of the risk you take today.

Resources

William J. Bennett, *The Book of Virtues* (New York: Simon and Schuster, 1993).

Tony Campolo, *Let Me Tell You a Story* (Nashville: Word, 2000).

ESTHER
TAKES A RISK
Esther 5:1-8; 7:1–8:2

Saints Who Took Chances

The heroes and heroines in the Bible took risks. Noah built an ark while the neighbors laughed; Abraham packed up everything he owned and headed for a place unknown to him; Ruth went with her mother-in-law when common sense said to stay home; David picked up five smooth stones when all the smart money was on Goliath; Hosea searched for his wife with a love that made no sense; Joseph married a woman whose child wasn't his; the disciples dropped what they were doing to follow Joseph's step-son; Zacchaeus gave half his money to the poor when a third seemed sufficient; Peter announced to those who imprisoned them, "We cannot but speak of what we've seen and heard." Those who followed God lost friends, lost jobs, and lost their lives. Queen Esther was also a reluctant heroine who risked her life.

I. Esther's Banquet Plan: Part 1 (5:1-8)

Three days after the Jews began their fast, Esther prepared to make her entrance. The king immediately remembered why he married her. He promised to do whatever she asked—even giving her up to half of the kingdom. (Four chapters back he got rid of a wife who wanted to be treated as an equal!)

Esther didn't reveal her motive too soon. "I'd like to have dinner," she said, "just you and me and your good friend Haman." Ahasuerus was easily angered, and people had to approach him with care. Esther put a lot of thought into her succession of dinners. She was bright as well as brave. She was waiting for the perfect timing. She planned to manipulate the king into a favorable response. Apparently she decided that the best way to extract something from Ahasuerus was to place him in a setting where alcoholic beverages were served.

What she needed—the reversal of a decree that he had personally signed—was a subject too delicate for her to approach directly. Instead, she planned to encourage Ahasuerus to commit himself repeatedly to giving her anything she wished. Once she had made it impossible for him to deny her request without losing face, she would ask him to save her people.

In the middle of a bottle of wine that first night, the king asked again, "Esther, what do you want? Even up to half of my kingdom, just ask."

Esther said she wanted to have dinner with the king and Haman once more the next night. Ahasuerus looked at his friend and shrugged as if to say, "Who knows what women are thinking?"

II. Haman's Murderous Plan (5:9-14)

Haman was beaming. The queen was clearly a big fan of his. She had twice invited him to a private banquet with the king. But as he left the palace, Haman saw Mordecai sitting there, still refusing to bow. It made him furious. He decided not to do anything just then, but he told his wife and friends about it.

His wife, who was not a gentle woman, could see that Mordecai was ruining everything for her husband. She suggested that Haman put an end to his frustration by building a seventy-five-foot gallows and asking the king to hang Mordecai on it. She thought it would make Haman feel better.

Haman loved this idea. It was a permanent answer to the Mordecai problem. Figuring there was no time like the present, he decided to talk to the king the next day.

III. The King's Plan to Honor Mordecai (6:1-13)

Things looked grim for Mordecai, but luckily, the king couldn't sleep that night. Out of all the options available to an emperor, he asked for a reading of the congressional record. Surely that would put him to sleep! Coincidentally (or maybe not), the reading chosen from the record detailed how Mordecai had saved the king from an assassination attempt.

The king asked what had been done for Mordecai and was likely surprised to learn that he had received no reward. Persian kings were usually extremely generous in rewarding those who had served them well. It's strange that this particular good deed had gone unnoticed by the king.

The king always asked for help when he needed an idea, so he asked who else was in the palace. Coincidentally (or maybe not), Haman had just walked in to speak to the king about the gallows for Mordecai.

When the king asked, "What can I do to honor a hero?" Haman thought, *That would be me*, so he described the greatest reward: "Royal robes, a royal horse, a royal crown, a prince leading the hero through the streets."

The king said, "That sounds great. Do everything you just said for Mordecai the Jew. Get to it right this minute."

Haman's jaw fell to the floor. He thought he was going to die (and he was about to be right). He had to lead the parade, calling out, "Thus shall it be done for the man whom the king wishes to honor."

He gritted his teeth and got through it. He ran home mortified, hoping no one had recognized him, but knowing that everyone had.

When Haman told his wife and friends all that had happened, they warned him, "If you're in a fight with Mordecai, you're going to lose." It's ironic that Haman's friends first realized what would happen. Gentiles made the statement that the Jews would survive long before the Jews themselves understood it.

IV. Esther's Banquet Plan: Part 2 (6:14–8:2)

Haman had to hurry off to the second night of Esther's progressive dinner. They were drinking heavily again when the king asked, "Esther, what do you want? Even to half of my kingdom."

This time she had an answer: "O King, this is what I want—my life and the lives of my people. I'm one of those scheduled to be killed."

The king sounded as clueless as usual when he asked, "Whose idea was this? Who is he? This is monstrous!"

Esther pointed to Haman and said, "It's him." Haman started shaking. The king's trusted advisor was doomed. The king, raging, stomped out to think for a moment. Haman begged Esther for his life. The arrogant, vindictive enemy of the Jews was sniveling for his life before the Jewish queen.

Haman was still hanging on to Esther when the king returned. Ahasuerus completely misunderstood: "Will you even molest the queen while I'm just around the corner?"

Esther didn't correct the king's mistake. All the blood drained from Haman's face. When someone suggested that the gallows were ready, the king, with magnificent irony, hanged Haman on the scaffold Haman had prepared for Mordecai. The king gave Haman's house to Esther and Haman's job to Mordecai.

Esther had grown from a passive girl to a powerful woman. Her people were saved because she rose above her fears and took a risk.

V. Taking Chances

Church history is filled with saints who, like Esther, took chances. Saint Francis gave up his material goods, taking his place with the poor; Martin Luther faced prison and announced, "My conscience is captive to the word of God. God help me. Here I stand"; Lottie Moon preached the gospel in China, praying for someone to respond; Dietrich Bonhoeffer returned to Germany to suffer with his people; Rosa Parks sat in the front of the bus when it would have been easier to move to the back; Oscar Romero stood for what the church could be even when he knew it might cost him his life. They took chances that didn't make their lives easy, but eventually improved circumstances for themselves and others.

God calls us to take risks, but most days we do only what we've always done. We do what's expected, and the expectations aren't much. For most of us, an ordinary day requires little courage. Fear keeps us from taking chances we didn't take yesterday.

What's the biggest risk you ever took for God? Most days we don't love our enemies. Most days we don't give sacrificially. Most days we don't take chances for what we know is true. Most days we don't show our love for God in surprising ways.

God calls us beyond the norms of everyday behavior. Most days we do what's ordinary. We compromise without thinking about it. We conform without considering the alternatives. We do what's expected as a matter of course. Trying something new doesn't occur to us. Paralyzed by fear isn't just a cliché. Sometimes we would be better off sorry than safe. Our dreams get set aside because of little fears.

It's easier to settle for an easy faith than to try to fulfill God's best hopes for us. We learn what others say about Christ without seeking Christ on our own. We repeat what we've heard about prayer without truly praying. We echo what we've learned about Scripture without studying it for ourselves. We learn how to repeat the answers without asking the questions. We memorize the map without taking the trip. Faith that merely accepts the beliefs of others is cowardly.

We try not to think about it, because we know that if we try to live with real courage, it won't be easy. C. S. Lewis said, "If you want a religion to make you really comfortable, I certainly don't recommend Christianity."

When our only prayer is "God, keep us safe," we aren't faithful to the gospel. God constantly offers possibilities. Often we feel the Spirit pulling us to do something rare, something good. The Spirit has a relentless spontaneity. Every once in a while, we should act on impulse with only the faintest impression that we heard God say, "Go." No day is without a unique opportunity. We must keep asking, "What courageous thing might God want from me?"

God will give us the courage to think new thoughts, change our minds, admit we've been wrong; to stop doing what we should have never started doing; to start doing what we should have always done; to put aside our own entertainment to do something good even though it's hard; to do our job well when it's easier to do only enough to get by; to be the one who says, "We can do better than this"; to love someone who doesn't love us; to say the name of Christ to someone who may not welcome it; to open ourselves to Scripture and ask God for guidance.

Ask God to make you brave and empty you of everything that's cowardly. You might end up speaking an extravagant word of grace to someone. Do something for your church that you've never done. Pick something that frightens you. Be part of a difficult ministry. Stand up for someone who's always being put down. Say boldly, "That's enough." Speak to someone at work whom you usually dismiss. Give more than it's easy to give. Go one step further than you've gone before. Be open to frightening possibilities. God may invite you to a new job, a surprising friendship, or a life in ministry.

How long has it been since you took a risk because you believe in God?

Notes

Notes

THE JEWS
PREVAIL

Esther 8:3–9:3, 26-28

Central Question

What victories do I need to celebrate?

Scripture

Esther 8:3–9:3, 26-28 8:3 Then Esther spoke again to the king; she fell at his feet, weeping and pleading with him to avert the evil design of Haman the Agagite and the plot that he had devised against the Jews. 4 The king held out the golden scepter to Esther, 5 and Esther rose and stood before the king. She said, "If it pleases the king, and if I have won his favor, and if the thing seems right before the king, and I have his approval, let an order be written to revoke the letters devised by Haman son of Hammedatha the Agagite, which he wrote giving orders to destroy the Jews who are in all the provinces of the king. 6 For how can I bear to see the calamity that is coming on my people? Or how can I bear to see the destruction of my kindred?" 7 Then King Ahasuerus said to Queen Esther and to the Jew Mordecai, "See, I have given Esther the house of Haman, and they have hanged him on the gallows, because he plotted to lay hands on the Jews. 8 You may write as you please with regard to the Jews, in the name of the king, and seal it with the king's ring; for an edict written in the name of the king and sealed with the king's ring cannot be revoked." 9 The king's secretaries were summoned at that time, in the third month, which is the month of Sivan, on the twenty-third day; and an edict was written, according to all that Mordecai commanded, to the Jews and to the satraps and the governors and the officials of the provinces from India to Ethiopia, one hundred twenty-seven provinces, to every province in its own script and to every people in its own language, and also to the Jews in their script and their language. 10 He wrote letters in the name of King Ahasuerus, sealed them with the king's ring, and sent them by mounted couriers riding on fast steeds bred from the royal herd. 11 By these letters the king allowed the Jews who were in every city to assemble and defend their lives, to destroy, to kill, and to annihilate any armed force of any people or province that might attack them, with their children and women, and to plunder their goods 12 on a single day throughout all the provinces of King Ahasuerus, on the thirteenth day of the twelfth month, which is the month of Adar. 13 A copy of the writ was to be issued as a decree in every province and published to all peoples, and the Jews were to be ready on that day to take revenge on their enemies. 14 So the couriers, mounted on their swift royal steeds, hurried out, urged by the king's command. The decree was issued in the citadel of Susa. 15 Then Mordecai went out from the presence of the king, wearing royal robes of blue and white, with a great golden crown and a mantle of fine linen and purple, while the city of Susa shouted and rejoiced. 16 For the Jews there was light and gladness, joy and honor. 17 In every province and in every city, wherever the king's command and his edict came, there was gladness and joy among the Jews, a festival and a holiday. Furthermore, many of the peoples of the country professed to be Jews, because the fear of the Jews had fallen upon them. 9:1 Now in the twelfth month, which is the month of Adar, on the thirteenth day, when the king's command and edict were about to be executed, on the very day when the enemies of the Jews hoped to gain power over them, but which had been changed to a day when the Jews would gain power over their foes, 2 the Jews gathered in their cities throughout all the provinces of King Ahasuerus to lay hands on those who had sought their ruin; and no one could withstand them, because the fear of them had fallen upon all peoples. 3 All the officials of the provinces, the satraps and the governors, and the royal officials were supporting the Jews, because the fear of Mordecai had fallen upon them.... 26 Therefore these days are called Purim, from the word Pur.

Thus because of all that was written in this letter, and of what they had faced in this matter, and of what had happened to them, 27 the Jews established and accepted as a custom for themselves and their descendants and all who joined them, that without fail they would continue to observe these two days every year, as it was written and at the time appointed. 28 These days should be remembered and kept throughout every generation, in every family, province, and city; and these days of Purim should never fall into disuse among the Jews, nor should the commemoration of these days cease among their descendants.

Reflecting

Josh Burton and Susie Ward lived in Pearlington, Mississippi. When they were seventy-five years old and widowed, they struck up a great friendship and, later, a great romance. On Monday morning, August 29, 2005, Josh and Susie awoke in Susie's home in a situation that they never anticipated: Hurricane Katrina had swept through their town and flooded the house.

By midday, Josh and Susie were clinging to a back porch post treading in more than ten feet of water. They prayed that God would somehow save them. Then, at the point of giving up, when Josh's crippled legs could no longer keep him afloat, a life jacket popped from below the surface and saved them. They clung to their bobbing house for the next six hours, and when the waters receded, it took rescuers three days to find them. They were taken to separate hospitals, one in Meridian and one in Jackson. Their families, thinking they were both dead, did not find them for two additional weeks.

As Josh and Susie were rescued, they made a promise: "If God will allow us to be reunited, we'll be married and finish our days together." They kept that promise. On a cold December afternoon, they spoke their vows in the front yard of their new home provided by Habitat for Humanity. More than a hundred volunteers—donors, designers, and carpenters—stood on the front porch as witnesses to and participants in a multifaceted celebration.

Twenty-five feet from their new home, caskets were still lying on top of the ground, burst open from the flooded cemeteries. Still, life was returning to that little town, and there was much to celebrate.

Studying

The story of Esther ends with a great celebration. The Jewish people are saved from Haman's genocidal plot through the intervention of Esther and Mordecai. While the edict to exterminate the Jews still hangs over the nation's head (by Persian custom, laws were not repealed), Esther succeeds in obtaining a second royal pronouncement: the Jews are allowed to defend themselves against any who would attempt to carry out Haman's plans.

King Ahasuerus, gracefully and somewhat passively, allows Esther and Mordecai to construct this new law in his name. The new edict is delivered throughout the Persian kingdom by royal couriers just as the previous orders had been (Esth 8:9, 13-14).

The author of Esther is deliberate in pointing out that Mordecai's new edict allowed for more than self-defense. The Jews are granted the right to annihilate any armed force that comes against them, and also to destroy the "children and women, and to plunder the goods" of their enemies (8:11). Esther 9:16 says that, in the aftermath of the Jewish defense, the Jews "killed seventy-five thousand of those who hated them; but they laid no hands on the plunder."

The wholesale killing of women and children is problematic, and this should be acknowledged rather than explained away. If we interpret Scripture through the lens of Christ, his example and teachings, we have a conflict that can only be resolved by stating that God had nothing to do with commanding these actions. Granted, these actions serve the intent of the author, who describes the great role reversal of redemption that has taken place for the Jewish people. The enemies coming to exterminate the innocent Jews, including their women and children, suffer the intended fate while the Jews escape. For the Jews, mourning and grief is turned to joy and celebration. A national tragedy is transformed into a national celebration. We should acknowledge the author's intention to celebrate Israel's triumph over its enemies, who reap the whirlwind of destruction. Yet we cannot hold God responsible for this command to slaughter the innocent, particularly in light of what we know about God through Jesus Christ.

In the aftermath of this violent defense, the Jews institute a national celebration to remind them of their redemption secured by Mordecai and Esther. The name given to the celebration was Purim, from the Akkadian word *pur*, which means "lot" or "chance."

Esther 3:7 explains that Haman cast the *pur* to determine the day of the Jewish genocide. He rolled the dice, spun the wheel, drew straws—choose your metaphor. He allowed "fate" to decide the date. In ironic fashion, the day set for destruction became a day of deliverance. Thus, Purim was the name assigned to the festival.

The Jews were no strangers to celebration. The Mosaic Law describes almost a dozen national celebrations. Some of these are as regular and simple as the Sabbath day. Others are observed more rarely, like the year of Jubilee, which occurred only once every fifty years.

All of the varied celebrations of Judaism are derived from the Mosaic Law except two: Purim and Hanukkah. Both of these emerged out of the difficult period after the Babylonian exile. As the Jewish nation stood on the brink of destruction, they were pulled from ruin and miraculously saved. The rescue by Esther was such a community-shaping experience that the celebration of this event was elevated nearly to the status of the high holy days of Mosaic tradition. Purim is rooted in the redemptive history of the Jewish people. The hallmarks of Purim are the exchanging of gifts, music and dancing, children dressed in colorful costumes, feasting, and joy.

As the book closes, Esther and Mordecai's heroic stature is forever remembered alongside the epic figures of Jewish history. But neither Esther nor Mordecai can take credit for the deliverance of the Jewish people, any more than Moses, Gideon, David, or Deborah could have in their day. It was God working all along, and while God did not part the waters or slay giants in the book of Esther, God was still bringing about redemption in concert with those who shared that higher purpose. Invoked or not invoked, God is present. This is reason enough to celebrate.

Understanding

Celebrations come in all shapes and sizes. Christmas, New Year's, birthdays, anniversaries, and Independence Day are all well known and expected. Other occasions are not as recognizable on the annual calendar, but just as significant for individuals: a high school graduation, a victory in a sports tournament, or a wedding engagement.

There are opportunities to celebrate when we sense that God has intervened in our lives, like the birth of a child, recovery from sickness, the restoration of a relationship, a "miraculous" escape from an automobile accident, or the safe return of a loved one from the theater of war. Events like these may not be institutional or national holidays, but for those who have experienced God as a "refuge and strength, a very present help in trouble" (Ps 46:1), grateful celebration is the only appropriate response.

For what, or whom, are you grateful? How can you properly celebrate these things or people as gifts from God? On the contrary, when difficult times come, how can you find ways to be thankful and celebrate even then?

The book of Esther teaches us to be mindful of those times when God has intervened on our behalf. Remember, God's name is never mentioned in the book of Esther. This is what we might call a "secular" book rather than a "sacred" one. Such distinctions, however, are misleading. God is not restricted by our definitions and categorizations. God is active and present in the world and in the lives of people. We may not see burning bushes, parting waters, or bread and fish feeding the multitudes, but this does not mean God is absent.

God's good pleasure is to work through people. Those who have eyes of faith recognize this and are not afraid to acknowledge it. Our eyes should always be open to discover God at work, and when we see it we should boldly celebrate.

What About Me?

• *Our eyes should be open to God's activity in our lives.* The silence of God in the book of Esther is normative for our lives as well. Rarely do we hear or see God's direct intervention. It is subtle, quiet, and restrained. Yet quietness does not equal absence. How has God gently worked in your life? In the life of your family? Your church?

• *Although we have many questions, our great hope is that life does not operate by chance.* God's control of the world has been long debated. Many say God is in absolute control of every detail of life, causing all that happens in our world. Others say God is absent and uninvolved, allowing the universe to dictate its own course. The balance is somewhere between. God has chosen to accomplish redemption by partnering with people. Thus life is not chance; it is a dance between the human and the divine. Where do you sense God's call to partnership?

• *We all have uncelebrated moments.* A near miss on the highway. An "all-clear" report from the oncologist. The arrival of a certain piece of news just in the nick of time. We all have had moments where certain disaster was averted at the last possible second. Do we stop to celebrate these moments? Do we direct our praise to God from whom all good things come?

• *Thankfulness is more than a one-day national holiday; it is a way of life.* Too often we reserve our gratefulness for "big" events or the occasional grace at the dinner table. Gratitude, however, is a lifestyle we must choose. The food we eat, the people we love, the church community of which we are a part, devoted friends, and years of good health are all gifts we can take for granted. What are you thankful for that you have overlooked? When was the last time you paused to thank God for the blessings of life? Let us daily commit ourselves to a life of thanksgiving, gratefully celebrating all that God has given.

Resource

Gene M. Tucker, "Esther, Book of," *The Oxford Companion to the Bible*, ed. Bruce M. Metzger and Michael D. Coogan (New York: Oxford University Press, 1993).

THE JEWS
PREVAIL

Esther 8:3–9:3, 26-28

The Drama

The most fun I ever had at youth camp (that didn't involve water balloons) was a Bible study on Esther. We presented the story as a melodrama with a hunky young king, a flirty Esther, a brave Mordecai in a white wig, and the evil Haman with a tiny fake mustache and a swastika. Just as when the Jews read the story at the festival of Purim, each time the storyteller said the name Haman, the crowd hissed, booed, and rattled noisemakers.

The audience laughed as the king ran around the theater frantically looking for a new queen. Esther exercised and had her eyebrows plucked. Haman (*hiss, boo, clickety-clack!*) kept insisting that everyone should bow before him. He threw big fuzzy dice to decide the day on which he would have the Jews killed.

The king was too busy looking in the mirror to pay attention, so he agreed to Haman's evil plan. Brave Mordecai told Esther she had to do something. She paced back and forth a few times before she agreed.

Esther put on expensive, uncomfortable shoes and went to the king. She fluttered her eyebrows and invited Hunky and Haman to a fancy dinner. Haman got bad advice from his wife, who had a brother in the gallows business.

A large volunteer played the royal horse as Haman led Mordecai, who was wearing a fine-looking bathrobe, around the stage to thunderous applause. The crowd was delighted when Haman grabbed the queen's ankles to beg for his life.

We made the right decision in not having teenagers act out either the hanging or the destruction of the Jews' enemies.

I. The Reversal (8:13-17)

If this were a Hollywood movie, the story could end after Haman's death. We could cut straight to the closing titles as the narrator intones, "And so Mordecai and Esther, and all the Jews in the kingdom of Ahasuerus, lived happily ever after."

Esther wasn't written for Hollywood. The lives of the Jews still hung in the balance because the king's proclamation was irrevocable. After the king had Haman hanged, Esther pled her case to Ahasuerus again. She wept as she begged the king to reverse the edict to kill the Jews. The king responded, "Do what you think makes sense. You write a law and I'll back it up."

The lawyers started working on the paperwork. They wrote as Mordecai dictated. This part of the story is less than uplifting. Not content with saving their people and removing Haman from the picture, Esther and Mordecai used their new power to orchestrate the slaughter of their enemies. (War is about as popular with religious people as it is with everybody else.)

The new edict allowed the Jews to defend themselves. What Haman had planned as a day of annihilation became a day of revenge.

II. The Revenge (9:1-17)

On the day that Haman had sought the Jews' destruction, the tables were turned as the Jews triumphed over those who hated them. They finished off their enemies, slaughtering them left and right. At the end of the day, the king told Queen Esther, "Here in the palace alone the Jews have killed five hundred, plus Haman's ten sons. Think of the killing that must have been done in the rest of the provinces. What else do you want? Name it and it's yours."

In a verse that doesn't get memorized during Vacation Bible School, Esther asked for another day for the Jews to massacre their enemies and for the bodies of Haman's ten sons to be hung in public display on the gallows (9:13). Across the empire, the Jews killed seventy-five thousand of their enemies.

Regarding this part of the story, J. E. McFadyen writes, "All the romantic glamour of the story cannot blind us to its religious emptiness and moral depravity." Nineteenth-century German scholar Heinrich Ewald said that when you come to Esther from the other books of the Old Testament, you "fall from heaven to earth" (Iain Duguid, "The Eschatology of the Book of Esther," *Westminster Theological Journal* 68 [2006]: 85).

We may feel embarrassed as we read of Israel's delight at the deaths of their enemies, but we must also admit that we love the moment when the villain finally receives justice, when James Bond or Jason Bourne or Harry Potter conquers his rival. We also long for the destruction of our enemies. Though we may be uncomfortable with the turn of events, the book of Esther celebrates the defeat of evil.

III. The Feast of Purim (9:18-32)

The triumph of the Jews seems like another appropriate place for the book's ending, but Esther includes a lengthy section after the conclusion of the action that describes the establishment of Purim.

The name itself is ironic. Haman had cast *pur*—lots—to choose the day on which to destroy the Jews, so they called the celebration Purim. In synagogues around the world, people who have been through the Holocaust celebrate a raucous holiday with music, drinking, and three-cornered cookies. The high point of the celebration is the reading of Esther. Jews celebrate victory over their enemies by feasting, rejoicing, and giving food to one another and presents to the poor.

IV. The Final Conclusion (10:1-3)

The series of conclusions continues with another curious detail— Ahasuerus raised taxes (10:1). The king, whose callous indifference allowed Haman's edict in the first place, seems untouched, still exercising power in his own interests. In the last recorded act of Ahasuerus, just as throughout the story, his personal benefit remained paramount, no matter the cost to his subjects. The more things change, the more they stay the same in the empire of Ahasuerus.

Esther is not a fairy tale that ends with the hero and heroine riding off into the sunset, destined to live happily ever after. The book closes with gratitude that God has lightened the people's darkness, but it still looks forward with longing eyes for the dawn of the promised new world.

Fortunately, Mordecai was now second in rank to Ahasuerus. The position once filled by the enemy of the Jews was now occupied by their friend. It was good news, but it wasn't the ultimate good news. Mordecai and Esther rose to positions of considerable influence and power, but ultimately the empire's power remained largely intact. In Esther's day, the complete fulfillment of God's hopes was yet to come. There is a measure of peace for the Jews, but not the final peace for all of God's people.

Even today, the enemies of goodness continue to win some battles, and good people often suffer greatly. Esther is more than a reminder of God's past ability to intervene in the lives of God's people. It also reminds us that we await a greater deliverance.

The celebration of Purim helped the people look forward to the day when their king would no longer be named Ahasuerus. The great reversal of the book of Esther is not yet the great reversal of all of history. It was a great deliverance, but one day the true King will bring a reign that will never end.

The Christian church has not commonly observed Purim, but maybe we should mark this unique celebration on our calendars and celebrate not just the victory of Esther, but an eternal kingdom yet to be.

God Is at Work

Much is made over the fact that Esther is the only book in the Bible without any mention of God. When Yogi Berra saw a player make the sign of the cross before he stepped into the batter's box, Berra said, "I think God should be allowed to just watch this one." Those who are offended by the violent nature of Esther may feel that God should be allowed to just watch Esther's particular story.

It is true that the story of Esther is told without any reference to God. The book could have been written for a newspaper. Reporters often give accounts of power plays, ethnic cleansing, and apparent coincidences that change the course of events without using religious language. Why did the author of Esther consistently avoid a direct reference to God? Maybe the Jewish people had begun to wonder if, after the many years of captivity, Yahweh was still present in their lives.

A string of "coincidences" was necessary to turn the story around and destroy Haman while saving the Jews. These are, for the author, God's work. God is always active, whether noted or not.

Not one of the remarkable turns in the story is attributed to God, however. As readers, we should be amazed at how everything seems to happen in the right place at the right time. The Jews did not believe events happened by chance. They recognized the hand of Yahweh.

The unseen God acted to save God's people. The "main characters" of the story, Mordecai and Esther, are not introduced until the middle of the second chapter, a fact suggesting that, however central they are to the immediate conflict, they are bit players in a much larger struggle. Bigger issues are at stake in the story than the happiness of individuals. Mordecai and Esther are the flesh-and-blood instruments God uses in fulfilling God's plan.

Both Jewish and Christian scholars insist that the primary theme of Esther is the providence of God. God is working out God's purposes in ways we cannot predict, understand, or explain. The world is sometimes seen as a closed system of cause and effect into which God does not penetrate. This is contrary to the biblical understanding of the way God works. We shouldn't limit God to miraculous, dramatic intervention and thus deprive ourselves of God's presence in our daily lives. God did not intervene "miraculously" in the life of Esther. Not one "miracle" is recorded in the book (Dave Bland, "God's Activity as Reflected in the Books of Ruth and Esther," *Restoration Quarterly* 24/3 [1981]: 141–47).

The truth for those who pay attention is that God is always at work. God is active in more ways than we recognize. God is loving people we've never met, healing the sick, caring for the lonely, helping all kinds of people learn to love each other.

Think about what God is doing as you read this commentary. God is helping you ask questions. God is offering you understanding. God is making you think about how the story relates to your life. When you read about the Jews' celebration, God calls you to celebrate.

God is forever pushing for the good, pushing us to faith, hope, and love. God is working for what is best for children, the elderly, the poor, and the lost. God is acting for the good of everyone everywhere. God is forever influencing, persuading, and inspiring. God is at work all day, every day. Someday we'll remember all the good we knew, turn to God, and say, "That was you. I should have known."

Wherever people live with compassion, God is there. God is at work in Sunday school teachers, loving grandparents, hopeful children, and any who have the courage to let God work through them.

Notes

Notes

nextsunday
STUDIES

1 Peter
Keep Hope Alive
This study of First Peter focuses on keeping hope alive in the face of pressures and circumstances that could possibly extinguish it completely, or worse, turn authentic faith into a pale replica of the real thing.

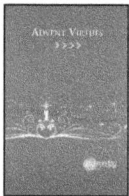

Advent Virtues
The phrase "holiday rush" is not an exaggeration. The frantic pace required to purchase gifts, bake holiday foods, and attend Christmas parties, plays, and performances takes its toll; we arrive at Christmas Day exhausted. Within the context of December busyness, the ancient Christian season of Advent takes on new meaning and acquires renewed importance. May God instill the virtues of *hope*, *peace*, *joy*, *love*, and *faith* in each of us this Advent.

Apocalyptic Literature
This study examines five apocalyptic texts in the Bible—from Zechariah, Daniel, Matthew, and Revelation. With each new year bringing a new prediction of impending doom, it is always a perfect time to get the story straight. Apocalyptic literature does not address the future. It addresses our present.

Approaching a Missional Mindset
The World isn't the same as it once was. We must be the church in a new place, in unimagined ways, and with a wider range of people. Engage your small group with the radical and refreshing challenge of developing a "missional lifestyle."

Baptist Freedom
Celebrating Our Baptist Heritage
What makes a Baptist a Baptist? Of course, the ultimate answer is simple: membership in a local Baptist church. But there are all kinds of Baptist churches! What are the spiritual and theological marks of a Baptist? What is the shape and the feel of Baptist Christianity?

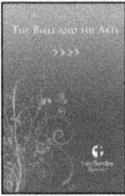

The Bible and the Arts
God has used artistic expression throughout the centuries to convey truth, offer blessing, and urge believers to deeper faithfulness. In modern life, artistic expression flourishes, from movies to books to music to paintings to photographs. Sometimes artists are intentional about trying to portray God's truths. Other times, perhaps God is working even when the artist is unaware of it. As believers, we may hear and see God at work in many art forms.

The Birthday of a King
The first four lessons in this unit draw inspiration from a traditional interpretation of the Advent candles as the Prophets' Candle, the Bethlehem Candle, the Shepherds' Candle, and the Angels' Candle. The final lesson, which occurs after Advent, celebrates the theological meaning of Jesus' birth as described in the prologue to John's Gospel.

Challenges of the Christian Life
The way of the cross is difficult, and taking Jesus seriously means looking honestly at how we fall short of God's best hopes for us and seeing how much we need God's grace. For all of us there are times when we need to remember that Christ is our saving grace and recommit ourselves to the journey of faith, rediscovering, again and again, the life-giving purpose described in the book of Ephesians.

Christ Is Born!
Even in the midst of difficult circumstances, Advent is a time when we can find hope. Much like today, people in the 1st century church faced struggles. Examining the Gospel of Matthew, lessons include "Waiting for Christ," "Preparing for Christ," "Expecting Christ," "Announcing Christ," and "The Arrival of Christ."

Christians and Hunger

These sessions challenge us to apply gospel lenses and holy imagination to what literally gives us energy to live: food. With God's grace, we have the opportunity to imagine communities where tables are large and all are fed.

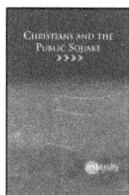

Christians and the Public Square

Politics and faith are tricky areas for Christians to negotiate. The First Amendment to the Constitution guarantees religious freedom for all Americans. As Christians who are also citizens, questions abound: How do we distinguish between faithful and unfaithful forms of civic engagement? How do we give Caesar his due while giving our all to God?

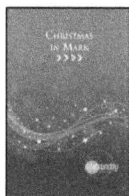

Christmas in Mark

In the early chapters of Mark, we will encounter a Christmas story. This story, however, will not be quite like the one told by other Gospel writers, but it will resonate with the reality of your life. Mark doesn't deny the beauty or reality of the nativity; however, he seems to believe that Christmas begins—the gospel begins—when Christ intrudes upon the hard realities of life.

The Church on a Mission

What does it mean to be a church on a mission? The lesson of Acts 1:8 is that we must simultaneously carry out Christ's mandate at home, in our region, in places that have been our blind spots, and around the world.

Colossians
Living the Faith Faithfully

Paul's letter to the Colossians begins with a high-minded philosophical defense of the faith, but concludes with a collection of extremely practical advice for living by faith. This study addresses the questions many Christians face today, helping them apply Paul's practical advice in their own lives.

Easter Confessions

Easter confession is often found on many different lips in the Gospel of John. When we listen carefully, those ancient confessions still echo into this new millennium.

Embracing the Word of God

We live during a time of transition in Christian history. Basic assumptions about the truth of the Christian faith are being questioned, not only by nonbelievers, but by Christians themselves. First John offers a starting point for understanding of what it means to "be" Christian.

Esther: A Woman of Discretion and Valor

The book of Esther is not a record of historical facts as such. Rather, it is a magnificent narrative that refuses to interpret life as being driven by coincidence or happenstance. In the otherwise unknown characters of Esther, Haman, and Mordecai, we trace the movement of the divine hand as God collaborates with God's risk-taking people to rescue them from the hand of their enemies.

Facing Life's Challenges

This study explores four significant challenges common to most persons of faith: the challenge of new light, the challenge of time's limit, the challenge of living with mystery, and the challenge of authentic spirituality. Although these issues are neither simple nor easy to ponder, this study effectively leads us in confronting these challenges.

Forgiveness and Reconciliation

Forgiveness is a central issue in our capacity to remain redemptively connected to those relationships we prize. Restoring broken or interrupted relationships is a primary issue for all of us, and managing forgiveness is crucial to the possibility of experiencing reconciliation. Several dimensions of forgiveness affect our lives in significant ways. In this study, we attempt to address a few of those important issues.

The Four Cardinal Virtures

Christians are learning how to distinguish between members of a church and disciples of Christ. Discipleship involves developing virtues in those who come to our churches seeking life, salvation, grace, mercy. If we want to have something to offer a world in desperate need, then we must return to virtues like discernment, justice, courage, and moderation. We must return to the hard and glorious work of making disciples.

Godly Leadership

Nehemiah was called to return to Jerusalem to lead in the sacred task of rebuilding the city's walls. Displaying characteristics often lacking in secular leadership—prayerful humility, a willingness to work with diverse teams, wisdom in confronting conflict, and a passion to stand with the powerless—Nehemiah offered his people a portrait of godly leadership that can still shape our own calls to lead nearly 2,500 years later.

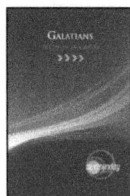

Galatians
Freedom in Christ

Paul wrote with fiery passion, as you will notice from the opening paragraphs of this letter to the Galatians. But his language reveals that he was writing about a crucially important issue—the very nature of salvation in Christ.

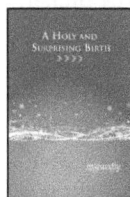

A Holy and Surprising Birth

Christmas begins here—discover these five love stories from the book of Luke and renew your appreciation of God's laborious effort to birth our salvation.

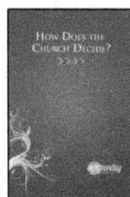

How Does the Church Decide?

An array of decisions draw energy and time from church members. These decisions may be theological, such as mode of baptism, aesthetic, such as the color of the sanctuary carpet, or functional, such as the selection of a new minister. This study will consider how the church has made its decisions in the past to help guide our decisions today.

Is God Calling?

Witness the varying forms of God's call, the variety of people called, and the variety of responses. Perhaps God's call to you will become clearer.

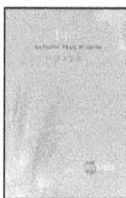

James
Gaining True Wisdom
If we'll be honest with God and ourselves as we study what James says, we can make great strides toward wisdom and a living faith.

Life Lessons from Bathsheba
Who was Bathsheba? She was a complex figure who developed from the silent object of David's lust into a powerful, vocal, and influential queen mother.

Life Lessons from David
In the Bible, we catch David in the various stages of the human journey: childhood, adolescence, adulthood, and senior adulthood. From the biblical treatment of the stages of David's life, we can land some insights to assist us in better understanding the human journey.

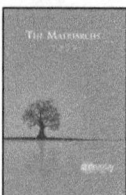

The Matriarchs
The matriarchs of Genesis offer their lives as a testimony of faith, perseverance, and audacity. We learn from their mistakes and suffering. We will gain the hope of Hagar, the joy of Sarah, and the audacity of Rebekah as we are challenged to examine our prejudices and our insecurities while studying Esau and Jacob's wives.

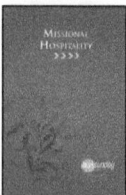

Missional Hospitality
If we are serious about following Jesus, we will be people of open hearts, open hands, and open homes. In other words, as followers of Jesus we will practice the fine art of hospitality. In lesson one, we reflect on hospitality to strangers. In lesson two, we address hospitality to the poor. In lesson three, we focus on hospitality to sinners. In lesson four, we learn about hospitality to newcomers. Lesson five reminds us about our hospitality to Christ.

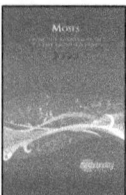

Moses
From the Burning Bush to the Promised Land
We would do well to trace the life of Moses so we might discover how his life changed, both personally and as Israel's leader, as he learned what it meant to love God with all his heart, soul, and strength.

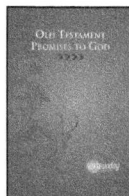

Old Testament Promises to God

Some individuals may feel that our promises couldn't possibly mean anything to God. Perhaps the real question is this: under what circumstances should or do we make such promises? The Old Testament contains several examples of people making promises to God, using the unique form of a biblical "vow."

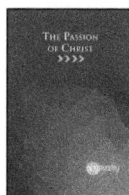

The Passion of Christ

The four lessons in this unit highlight the faith struggles of the early disciples. In lesson one, Jesus addresses the issues of faith and practice. In lesson two, we meet Judas who, like us, struggled with God's Kingdom and human kingdoms. In lesson three, the issue of temptation reminds us that our faith journey is a constant challenge. Lesson Four invites us to remember Peter's experience of "faith failure." Peter's failure, however, is not the final word. There is forgiveness.

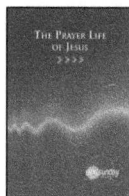

The Prayer Life of Jesus

The study of Jesus' prayer life can deepen our own prayer practices. These five sessions examine the importance of prayer at various stages of Jesus' life and ministry. He made no important decisions without consulting God.

Prepare the Way

In these sessions, we will seek to prepare the way toward and into the Christmas season. We begin with the theme of hopeful watchfulness in light of the coming of Christ. Next, we will spend two sessions considering the ministry of John the Baptist, the forerunner of Christ. Then, we will consider Matthew's account of the birth of Jesus and join in wonder at the miracle of "God with us." Finally, we will remember the story of the "holy innocents" killed by Herod in his attempt to eliminate the Christ child's threat to his power.

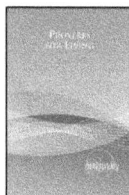

Proverbs for Living

Long ago, a collection of wise teachers committed themselves to the ways of God and collected this wisdom into what we know as the book of Proverbs. These four lessons explore the simple truth of Proverbs: there is a good life to be had—a life lived in faithfulness to God.

Qualities of Our Missional God

Too often we are tempted to let "numbers" drive missions. The book of Numbers reminds us that missions is motivated by something deeper. Missions reflects the heart and nature of God. If we can just get past the math, we can see God's nature clearly in the book of Numbers. . . in the wilderness.

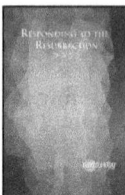

Responding to the Resurrection

All major events of human history elicit responses as varied as the personalities and situations represented by those affected. No one witnesses a world-changing event without being affected in some way. Studying the response of early followers helps us to shape our own response to the resurrection of Jesus. Each of us must consider our response to Jesus' life, teachings, death, resurrection, and call on our lives.

The Seven Deadly Sins

What exactly is sin? Just as we organize our cupboards and our schedules to make sense of our lives, Christian thinkers have organized sin into a number of categories in order to understand and surrender these patterns to God. The notion of "seven deadly sins" emerged as a way to recognize specific dangers to our spiritual lives. The purpose of the book is to guide people away from sin and into a wise and godly life.

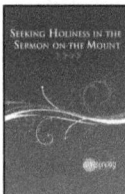

Seeking Holiness in the Sermon on the Mount

The Sermon on the Mount has long been recognized as the pinnacle of Jesus' teaching. But with this importance in mind, it's easy to think of Jesus' teachings as lofty and idealistic, offering little guidance for everyday life. Perhaps Jesus' sermon allows us to see beyond ourselves, beyond our own failures and shortcomings—revealing God's intention for our lives.

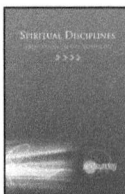

Spiritual Disciplines
Obligation or Opportunity?

The spiritual disciplines help deepen a believer's faith and increases his or her intimacy with Christ. In this study, we take a deeper look at some of the disciplines and consider their practice as a response to God's love.

Sing We Now of Christmas

In this study, we will explore some familiar prophecies, as well as the Gospel birth narratives, through the lens of five traditional Christmas carols. As carols have grown to be a fuller and more meaningful part of our worship and celebration, so too can the stories of Jesus' birth continue to grow within us and enrich our faith experience.

Stewardship
A Way of Living

Great News! Stewardship is not about money! At least not *just* about money. Certainly, stewardship relates to money, and, yes, we need to tithe. However, stewardship branches out into multiple areas of life. Properly practiced, this act of service can lead to peace and purpose in living.

The Ten Commandments

When the Ten Commandments are in the news, it is usually because a judge or teacher has hung them up on the walls. The Ten Commandments do not need to be posted or even preached nearly so much as they need to be practiced and viewed as life-giving, joyful affirmations of a better way of life.

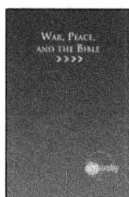

War, Peace, and the Bible

As people of faith, we are faced daily with an expectation that we participate in violent actions, our willingness to allow violence in the world to continue, and our response to violence in our lives. Is there a place for war and violence in our faith?

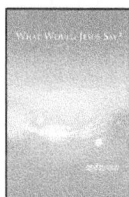

What Would Jesus Say?
A Lenten Study

To address what Jesus would say, we need to discover what Jesus did say. These lessons will attempt to help us understand Jesus' teachings and apply them today.

The Wonder of Easter

In 1 Corinthians 15, Paul asserts that the message that Jesus died for our sins, was buried, and rose on the third day is "of first importance" (v. 3). It is the core of the gospel story and of the Christian faith. But as much as Easter is a mystery to contemplate, it is also a hope to embrace and good news to proclaim.

**NextSunday Studies
are available from**

www.ingramcontent.com/pod-product-compliance
Lightning Source LLC
Chambersburg PA
CBHW070540030426
42337CB00016B/2288